Endorsements

"Many years ago, I met John Edelmann at a business breakfast. The Lord told me to sit next to "that Canadian dude" and told me to ask him this: "Do you want to stay here and listen to the guest speaker for the day or do you want to go have a coffee and hear what the Lord wants to say to you?" *(I had never done this before or since.)* And so our journey together began. Since then, we have been friends and fellow-adventurers in the marketplace, and sometimes in the church. I began Kingdom Builders and John E. began Kingdom Works International, and now "that Canadian dude" is back on his journey and *sold out and all in* for the extreme life God has called him to live. I can testify that the journey he has written about here is the absolute truth. May it bless and challenge you! Wake up, sons and daughters of the Living God, take heed, and go fulfill your own assignments in the kingdom!"

— Apostle John Lockwood
Founder of Kingdom Builders

"Many generations have had a mere copy of the true gospel ministered in a traditional manner with a very man-centered approach to the "church" as an institution. However, there have also been a remnant of consistently faithful believers who have been filled with the Holy Spirit and power. They have sought and loved Jesus with all of their heart, and have been focused on *knowing Jesus* and the power of His resurrection!

The purpose of a Jesus-centered gospel message and sacrificial lifestyle has been to express to the world the uncompromising heart and mind-changing love of God to a people who are going headlong into everlasting darkness without Him. This rescue, this mission, is at the very core of God's heart. This book addresses the realities of God's love and power and victory. It opens the door and urges you to ask God the real question: *What if I did this?*

If you could have anything at your disposal in the kingdom of God, anything that would change your life and change the lives of maybe millions of others, or even just one other, what would you do? Would you say, *"Father, what if...?"* Would you listen for His direction and go ahead?

May the impossible be made possible as you read this book!

> And Jesus answered saying to them, "Have faith in God. Truly I say to you, whoever says to this mountain, 'Be taken up and cast into the sea,' and does not doubt in his heart, but believes that what he says is going to happen, it will be granted him" (Mark 11:22-23, NASB).

We can all have an extreme walk with Jesus, never settling for second best!"

— Apostle Gary Hannie
Gary Hannie Ministries

STILL
STANDING

An Extreme Walk with Jesus,
Don't Settle for Second Best

JOHN EDELMANN

ISBN: 978-0-646-81152-9

Dedication

First and foremost, I want to dedicate this book to Abba Father and my Lord and Savior, Jesus Christ, my King of Kings and Lord of Lords, my Rock, my Salvation, and to the Holy Spirit who dwells in me. Thank You, my Lord, for taking me from a place of perpetual hopelessness and despair to a new and extreme life in You. You have given me a hope and a future; I can only repay You with my life. Thank You, Jesus.

I also dedicate this book to my beautiful wife, Angie. I thank God daily for her. She has been transformed by Him, and her heart is to serve Him. Angie, I love you more than words can say! Thank you for answering the call of God on your life, for such a time as this. The nations are calling us. God, I thank you for Angie coming into my life.

I also dedicate this book to my boys: Daniel, Shane, Christopher, Aaron, and Jordan, their better halves, and my grandchildren, Aiden, Isaiah, Malachi, Keira, Mia, Ariah, and one more about to arrive, another boy. My prayer is that "as for me and my house, we shall serve the Lord."

To my mom, Irene Edelmann: You have always supported me, no matter what. Thank you for your years of praying. Mom, I love you so much. I could never have had better parents. You have always been amazing. To my Dad who has passed, I could never have had a better earthly father, you were a champion in my eyes.

To my sisters and families, I love you and thank God for you all.

To one of my best friends, Wayne Schreck: When we met seventeen years ago, I never thought I would meet your daughter so many years later and she would become my wife! I thank you for your friendship all the years that we've spent together. Cheers, mate!

And to Louisa Groves, thank you for your daughter. She has been an incredible blessing.

Acknowledgments

F irst and foremost, I want to thank my wife, Angie. I don't know what this book would even look like without her standing beside me. Angie, you are my heart's desire, and I am not just thankful for you, I am more in love with you today than when we first met and I am so grateful for you! I am so proud of you and I thank the Lord for you daily!

I speak about **Pastor Graham Harris** a lot because I was blessed that the Lord put him into my life. He is an amazing man of God. I honor and thank you for all the time you spent mentoring, equipping, and teaching me, but most of all, for being my spiritual father. You watched me go from glory to glory to glory for twenty-six years. You probably asked the Lord from time to time, "Lord, why me?" The Lord has a sense of humor. Thank you, Pastor Graham. Most of all, I truly loved riding together, and our one-on-one time. I love you, man. Without your help, this book would never have been written.

Apostle John Lockwood and I met through a divine appointment, but that makes sense now that I know him. His life is one long series of divine appointments. He finds himself sitting with influential people on a regular basis. He is a man of great wisdom, revelation, understanding, and integrity. It is an honor to call him a friend. He has been there for me, not necessarily with answers, but always as an awesome listener. We are still waiting to see why the Lord connected us so long ago. John, you are an amazing friend and a blessing to me.

Sold out to the Lord and 100% in, **Apostle Gary Hannie** is a man of no compromise, a true disciple of Christ. He is called to a nation where persecution is an everyday threat, yet he will not deny Christ or water down the Word for anyone, no matter the cost. I have seen his resolve grow and grow, and I am honored to have him speak into my life. Pastor Gary and his wife, Cola, are truly amazing people whom the Lord uses greatly. Thank you for the way you have blessed and encouraged me.

Apostle Dorian (Doz) Ballard though I've only known him a short time, this man has truly passed the test of time. He has an incredible gift of teaching and is determined to teach the true gospel and to make disciples. He is determined to expose all false doctrine to the glory of the Lord. I can truly call him a mighty man of God and friend, he is uncompromised in all that he does. Praise the Lord.

David Burr and May Wan Khor are the most faithful husband and wife team I have ever seen. For over ten years, they opened up their boardroom to sixty to 120 people every Wednesday, blessing them with a Chinese banquet. They have sowed into speakers from all over the world as well as all the others who attended these weekly events. Always helping people who found themselves in trouble, David and May Wan modeled the hand of God blessing others in ways of which I do not think they are even aware. I have never seen such faithful and giving people in my life, and I admire and honor them both. May God bless you and enlarge your territory! You both deserve it. You are amazing people. Thank you for being a part of my life.

Although I only knew **Apostle John Tunnis** briefly, it was an honor and privilege to learn from him for that season. John's teaching gift left me bewildered at times, wondering, *How did he get that? I have read that verse so many times, but the revelation he brings is amazing.* This is a man who loves God. Bless you, mate.

The late **Pastor Keith Loft** was a mighty man of God. When I met him, I was young in the Lord, and he always guided me with a sure hand. As we spoke, he would say, "John, what does the Word say? John, if it doesn't line up with the Word, it is not God." My reply would be, "Yeah but—" to which he would interrupt me and say, "Yeah, *but nothing*! If it doesn't line up with the Word, *it is not God*." Pastor Keith was an awesome man of God who was not moved by circumstances or the natural; it was the Word or nothing. What a great man! It was a privilege to know him and have him speak into my life.

Though younger than I am, this guy has hit legendary status in my life. When I first came to Australia, I met Pastors Graham and **Pastor Peter Curtis**. Pastor Peter was a pastor under Pastor Graham and still is today. (They are faithful men who have been working together for twenty-five plus years.) I arrived here with two kids, three suitcases, and nothing else, so I would not let anyone in my home; but persistent Peter kept offering to come over to study the Bible with me. He came over after work and spent hours teaching me the Word. Pastor Peter, you are by far one of the greatest men of God I know. I thank you for the hours you put into me. Today I can say that because of your persistence, I am who I am in Him. Well done, my friend.

Contents

Foreword

John Edelmann has written this book as a testament to God's forgiveness, love, and faithfulness. I have known John for over twenty-six years now and have had the privilege of bringing him into the realm of God's kingdom of love, grace, and mercy. It has been a real joy to see John remain faithful—even through severe trials and testing.

Seven years ago John was released as a pastor. He has been involved in my church since 1993, and has walked with me in the mission fields of Malaysia and Indonesia for many years. John is *still standing* strong today. I highly recommend this book as a testimony of a man who has proven the faithfulness of God and the leading of the Spirit in his life. I still have the joy of speaking into John's life as a spiritual father and we enjoy time together, sharing the great things of God's kingdom with one another.

— Apostle Graham Harris
Senior Minister and Founder
I AM House of Worship, Melbourne, Australia

Chapter One: What If?

What if I told you that you could believe for more?

What if I told you that you could step into a new level of spiritual maturity and efficiency?

What if you could move from focusing on this life and self, into a focus that shifts to striving for the presence of God in every moment of every day?

What if there was a book that could challenge you to move out beyond your comfort zone to do exploits for the kingdom of God like you never could have imagined?

What if I could show you how to garner courage to look into a spiritual mirror in order to make changes that will have heavenly (or kingdom) results?

What if you were equipped to not only survive, but *thrive* in this world and walk in your destiny?

What if you could glimpse not just what you believe is your destiny in Christ, but what your *extreme destiny* is?

What if you could cast off the things that have held you back, shrug off second-best living and have an *extreme walk* with the Lord?

Are you ready to take a journey with me? This journey began with the Lord telling me that I would write a book (actually He said "books.") For me, I guess it starts with a dream, a commission, and a mandate.

The Dream: I saw thousands, tens of thousands, hundreds of thousands, millions of people falling into hell.

The Commission: I woke up at two in the morning hearing these words: "I commission you to go to the nations, go to the nations! Preach. Save My people! Go now!"

(The Dream and the Commission happened seventeen years ago.)

The Mandate was 2 Timothy 4:1-5: "Preach the Word":

> I solemnly charge you in the presence of God and of Christ Jesus, who is to judge the living and the dead, and by His appearing and His kingdom: preach the word [as an official messenger]; be ready when the time is right and even when it is not [keep your sense of urgency, whether the opportunity seems favourable or unfavourable, whether convenient or inconvenient, whether welcome or unwelcome]; correct [those who err in doctrine or behaviour], warn [those who sin], exhort and encourage [those who are growing toward spiritual maturity], with inexhaustible patience and [faithful] teaching. For the time will come when people will not tolerate sound doctrine and accurate instruction [that challenges them with God's truth]; but wanting to have their ears tickled [with something pleasing], they will accumulate for themselves [many] teachers [one after another, chosen] to satisfy their own desires and to support the errors they hold, and will turn their ears away from the truth and will wander off into myths and man-made fictions [and will accept the unacceptable]. But as for you, be clear-headed in every situation [stay calm and cool and steady], endure every hardship [without flinching], do the work of an evangelist, fulfill [the duties of] your ministry (2 Timothy 4:1-5 AMP).

Taking on the daunting project of writing this book seemed overwhelming. My thought was: *Lord, how do I convince the body of Christ, Your Body, to believe for more? What do I do to see Your people saved?* We, as a whole, are so caught up in the things of this world, that we do not see the Big Picture. This book was written to challenge, correct, warn (or rebuke, in other translations), exhort, encourage, teach, and bring truth. Ephesians 4:11-12 clearly states that the purpose of the apostle, prophet, evangelist, pastor, and teacher is the *equipping* of the saints for the work of the ministry. Why are the churches so full of people sitting there doing nothing for five, ten, fifteen, and even twenty years? Those called to the fivefold ministry gifts are to bring the body (the saints) to maturity, equip, and release them into the harvest field, their harvest field. We, as disciples of Christ, are to share our faith with those who do not know the soon and coming King: Jesus. We are to be lights in the darkness, not blend in with it. I start this chapter and the next with a list of challenging questions, my *what ifs. These questions are not meant to be condemning or judgmental. Their purpose is to stir our hearts and make us think.* However, if one was to feel convicted, then they should seek the Holy Spirit about the issue at hand. As the Word says, it is the Holy Spirit who brings conviction and not man (John 16:8-11). I believe this book was inspired by the Holy Spirit to challenge and encourage us to rise into the maturity of Christ and fulfill our destinies. Each and every person has a destiny and a purpose (Jeremiah 29:11); my heart is to stir the giftings and see everyone walk in his or her calling to the glory of God, to give the Lord our all (to be all in, 100%), and to want and expect more than just existing. I pray this book will stir your hearts to want to walk in **an extreme walk with Jesus, not settling for second best.** There is so much more for us in Christ. Both Angie (my wife) and I pray this book will speak to everyone who reads it and that it will glorify the Lord. So let's get started.

What if we could get past ourselves? You know—that I, me, me, I syndrome. *What if* we could get past seeking the *presents* and seek the *presence* of God? *What if* we could get past the flesh and walk in the fullness of the Spirit? Is that even possible? The Word says it is:

> I say then: Walk in the Spirit, and you shall not fulfill the lust of the flesh (Galatians 5:16).

Isn't that pretty clear? But something awful has happened in the church. There are many believers who go to church but do not walk in the Spirit of God. They have been taught that the Holy Spirit and His gifts are not for today. They have been told that being filled with the Spirit of God is not important. Meanwhile, the Word tells us we need "fresh oil" daily. Otherwise we walk in dead religion instead. Theologians argue the point, while the people of God languish. Dead religion leads only to hopelessness and despair.

I recently had lunch with a pastor in Bryan, Texas. He was adamant that when you gave your life to the Lord you were automatically filled with the Spirit. That would have been nice and many people are, but that does not happen to everyone, and it did not happen to me. Everything he said was like a challenge from what he learned during his time in seminary, yet for everything he countered me with in that conversation, the Holy Spirit gave me answers. It was amazing. The other two people present were embarrassed and felt I was being attacked by this guy to the point that they wanted to leave. However, the Holy Spirit was there, giving me all the answers I needed. I even gave him examples, like the one found in Acts 8:14-17. Phillip had led many to the Lord and then the apostles came later, after they heard that these new believers were not Spirit-filled and they came and laid hands on them, so they would receive the Holy Spirit. Next, the pastor noted that I had no formal training and he was a theologian, a scholar. Weren't some of the apostles fishermen with no education? And yet the Word says this of Peter and John when they stood before the Sanhedrin:

> Now when they saw the boldness of Peter and John, and perceived that they were uneducated and untrained men, they marvelled. And they realized that they had been with Jesus (Acts 4:13).

In the end, this pastor could not wait for our lunch to end and left quickly. My point? Walking as a Christian who believes but does not have the Spirit is a difficult road, extremely hard.

CHAPTER ONE: WHAT IF?

I was born on the west coast of Canada and gave my life to the Lord just before the first of my five sons was born in 1986. My friends John and Jacqueline led me to the Lord, but I was not Spirit-filled for seven years, and I only went to church once, perhaps twice. In 1993 I was living in Calgary, Alberta, Canada with my wife and five boys. I was a courier at the time, and just sick and tired of my life. I cried out, "Lord, if You are real, take me to Australia and I will stop everything I am doing, and I will serve You! Otherwise I am going to kill myself!" Then I applied to go to Australia. Four days later, I had clearance to go to Australia; and thirty days later, two of my sons were with me in Melbourne, Australia. I will fill in the blanks as we go, but this is where my life got turned upside down. Shortly after arriving in Melbourne, I prayed, "Lord, I believe You brought me here for a purpose and a reason. Show me where I am supposed to be." Long story short: I ended up attending a service at the Werribee City Church. I was uneasy from the first. Everyone was happy, dancing, singing, praising God. All I could hear in my head was: *Get out of here! These people are all nuts!* Every time I was going to grab my boys to bolt, the music stopped and I thought: *I can't go now.* This went on for what seemed to be an eternity (literally) and nearly everything in me said, *Run! Run now!* (I had very little church experience prior to this.) Finally, the music stopped, and a dude came to the front and began like this: "I believe the Lord is saying there are some people who need to come to the front. *Oh, man!* Everything in me screamed, *No! Don't do it!* but I was strangely drawn. A guy sitting beside me and my sons said, "Mate, I think that is you." I thought, *I am not your mate*, but answered, "What for?" He just said, "I believe you need to go up there." I asked him, "What about my boys?" He said, "I will watch them for you." The war going on in my head at that moment was one of the wildest battles I have ever had, and I was just about to have the most amazing experience of my life. I went up. There I was, standing in front of all those people, not knowing one person, and my boys were sitting with a complete stranger. I was standing in the middle of the building in front of the stage and there was a woman on my right and one on my left as well. I had never done this before. Thoughts raged through my head; my brain was howling. This dude went up to this lady on my left, prays for her, and she hit the floor, then the next one. I was thinking… (Well, maybe I won't share what I was thinking).

I was next. The man came up to me, and I was still thinking, *Run!* He introduced himself (I now know you don't call an apostle a dude, but I had to start somewhere). Pastor Graham Harris led me through the sinner's prayer, which I had done before (with really no results). *Okay, I did not see this coming!* Pastor Graham raised his hand to pray for me, and his hand was about six to eight inches from my head, and bam, I was on the floor. That was a first for me, and I was thinking, *What happened?* As soon as I could think that, it started. A wave went over me: I felt this super-intense wave come in from the top of my head and leave through the soles of my feet. It was like a surge, a major surge of electricity, and it freaked me out. It was followed by another, and then another, and yet another. I was so freaked out. I had never ever experienced anything in my life like this before (and I had had some pretty wild experiences in my life before this). I tried getting up but I was pinned to the floor; then on the fourth or fifth wave, everything changed. It was amazing.

I felt the waves turn and, for the first time in my life, I experienced wave after wave of peace and joy, and then love. It was the most incredible feeling I had ever experienced. I tried to get up again, but was still pinned to the floor. I thought of my boys, but for a while I was just lost in the moment as I was truly experiencing God the Father for the first time. I could have stayed down there longer but I fought it because I was now aware of my surroundings. I could hear Pastor Graham preaching. As I was getting up I thought, *Wow, all these people are looking at me,* and I felt embarrassed. I sat down beside my boys and the other guy (his name was Paul and we became good friends). I looked at him and said, "How embarrassing!" He said, "What is?" I said, "The dude didn't even touch me, and I fell on the floor. I must have been down there ten to fifteen minutes." Paul smiled and looked at his watch, "Mate, you were down there nearly an hour!" To this day, it has been the most intense experience I have ever had, and it was the day I met the Lord. After seven years I was filled with the Holy Spirit and my journey truly started. My quest for His presence, my quest for a closer and more intimate walk with Him began. Every day, as I bask in His glory, I say, "More, Lord, more; I know there is so much more." Angie and I get up every morning and sit with the Lord for two or three hours (and on a good day, even longer) before we do anything. The love of our Father, His tangible presence, and His glory is truly amazing, and can be had by anyone who thirsts and hungers after Him. More on that later.

I realized over time that I was walking in the steps that had been prepared beforehand. It took time, but I began to study the Word of God. It changed my life. Here are three of my favorite Scriptures. These three stand out and resonate in my spirit, and when I preach, I use them all the time. They seem to speak to the saved and unsaved alike.

> Your eyes saw my substance, being yet unformed. And in Your book they all were written, the days fashioned for me, when as yet there were none of them (Psalm 139:16).

Amazing! This is something to think about. Do we really understand what this means? We all have a book in heaven! *Our every day is written in it;* our future is ready for us to step into and embrace.

> "For I know the plans I have for you," declares the Lord, "plans to prosper you and not to harm you, plans to give you hope and a future. Then you will call on me and come and pray to me, and I will listen to you. You will seek me and find me when you seek me with all your heart. I will be found by you," declares the Lord, "and will bring you back from captivity" (Jeremiah 29:11-14a NIV).

Wow, what a promise! This is crazy; God has plans for me and you, and they are good!

> And we know that all things work together for good to those who love God, to those who are called according to His purpose (Romans 8:28).

Bad things do happen to good people, but God will use the bad for good, even though at the time, one could not see how this could possibly happen. When I look back over my life now, I can see how Abba took the bad things that happened in my life and has used them for good.

So why I am I writing this book? I have four reasons.

First, I have been led by the Spirit (the Holy Spirit) to write, so I write out of obedience.

Second, I want to equip the saints for the work of the ministry, as outlined in Ephesians 4:11-12. I want to stir the hearts of everyone who reads this to the truth that Abba has called every one of us to fulfill a mission (our destiny). We all are called to do something for Him through Jesus and the Holy Spirit. Nowhere in the Bible does it say this: "Get saved and sit here in the pew and wait till I come back!" On the contrary, the Word is clear, Jesus said this:

> And then He told them, "Go into all the world and preach the Good News to everyone" (Mark 16:15 NLT).

and

> And Jesus came and spoke to them, saying, "All authority has been given to Me in heaven and on earth. Go therefore and make disciples of all the nations, baptizing them in the name of the Father and of the Son and of the Holy Spirit, teaching them to observe all things that I have commanded you; and lo, I am with you always, even to the end of the age" Amen (Matthew 28:18-20).

Amen means "so be it." This is clearly not a "Hey man, if you're up to it" kind of request. No, *"so be it" is a final directive*. The purpose of the church is to equip the saints for what? The work of the ministry!

What if we all did the work of the ministry? I am hearing brakes skidding out of control here! Wait a minute! I am not called to preach, I am not called to travel, I am not an apostle, prophet, evangelist, pastor, or teacher. Jesus' answer comes swiftly: That may be the case, but you are all called to share the good news of Jesus crucified on the cross, risen three days later, and now seated at the right hand of God! Jesus: our Savior, Healer, Redeemer, Deliverer. *We are to share our testimonies of what He has done for us! You may be the only opportunity your workmate, hairdresser, dentist, banker, school teacher, and so on, will ever get to hear of the One and only Savior.*

> And they overcame him by the blood of the Lamb and by the word of their testimony, and they did not love their lives to the death (Revelation 12:11).

Sometimes, as Christians, we don't even have to speak! If we are truly transformed and led by the Holy Spirit, our witness speaks volumes. You know those times: You are at work and someone has told a dirty joke and you don't laugh with everyone else. Maybe only one person sees and recognizes there is something different about you, but *that one person counts*. Or when people are gossiping about others and you don't join in. I used to swear a lot. One day I was challenged. Someone asked me if I would swear if Jesus was standing beside me. I said no. "What if I was standing beside Pastor Graham?" Once again I said no. This left me thinking: *If I could control my swearing habit around the pastor, I should be able to control it anywhere. Self-control is a fruit of the Spirit.* So let's take Pastor Graham or your pastor, and Jesus out of the equation for a minute. If you are Spirit-filled, the Holy Spirit dwells within you. He is God! Just out of reverence to the Holy Spirit alone, we should not allow coarse jesting or foul language to come from our mouths (Ephesians 5:3-4). Those in the world watch to see a difference in Christians. Today people tell me that they would never have taken me for a preacher or a Christian based on my appearance. I look like what I am: a biker with tattoos and a handlebar mustache. At my last place of employment, I led two people to the Lord and was sharing with an atheist and others. Everywhere I go, I look for an opportunity to be used by the Lord. Am I special? No, definitely not. I am only available to the Holy Spirit; I earnestly seek to be used by the Lord daily.

And the third reason? I was sitting in my living room roughly seven years ago, having my morning time with the Lord, my coffee with Jesus. This has been a daily thing for 1fifteen to twenty years or so. I just talk with the Lord, worshipping and praising Him. I said, "Lord, I read Your Word and I love it. However, I have a problem when I read Your Word. All I see is story after story of all these people who have done great exploits for You. Lord, if I have to sit in church and hear one more boring sermon, just give me a noose. I used to lead an extreme and sometimes crazy (maybe more stupid than crazy) life in the world. Lord, if You cannot give me an *extreme life* like I read about in Your Word, please take me home (heaven, not Canada)."

Okay, here is a word of wisdom for you. When you share this with your senior pastor, and you include the part about having to listen to one more boring sermon, *maybe leave that bit out!* Fortunately, Pastor Graham has a great sense of humor. By this point, he had been my pastor, spiritual father, mentor, friend, mate, and confidant for eighteen-plus years and he still speaks into my life. So anyway, I had to retract the boring preaching bit, as Pastor Graham did about eighty percent of the preaching. He is an awesome preacher: a funny, witty, and incredible man of God. Amazingly, he knew what I was talking about; he had watched me for years. I was not being callous or flippant in what I said; I was serious. The cry of my heart was, "Lord, use me greatly for the expansion of the kingdom (seeing people saved and equipped) or please take me home." *My pastor understood.*

This is when my prayers changed and I started to pursue the Lord in even a greater way. My heart burned to walk in the fullness of the Lord; the mundane became unbearable. I said, "Lord, I want an *extreme walk* with You or nothing." The answer was in dying to self to become who He had called me to be; and believe me, this is a work in progress, as we all are. Our goal is to deny ourselves and take up the cross daily. What is *extreme living?* It is a state in which you surrender everything to the Lord: your will, your ways, your thoughts, everything; and then you say, "Lord, *Your will* be done in my life on earth as it is in heaven. You kill the flesh daily and take up your cross and follow Him wholeheartedly.

You go where He tells you to go, and say what He tells you to say and do what He tells you to do, without hesitation. You go into the world and preach the gospel in your sphere of influence (your workplace, your gym, your school, your community). This is *extreme living*. The Lord is at the center of your life and everything you do is about pleasing Him. Is it possible to live like this? Yes! Is it easy? No, it requires constantly coming before Him, but we can do all things through Christ who strengthens us. We can only do this through the Holy Spirit. Here are some examples of extreme living from the Bible.

Look at Gideon. Here is a guy with 32,300 with him up against an innumerable army. The Lord says, "Yo, Gideon, you have *too many* men there. Tell those who really don't want to be here (who are afraid and fearful) that they can go home. So 22,000 men take a hike. Gideon was just a man, so there is a strong chance he may have thought, *Wow, Lord, I didn't see that coming! Astronomical odds before 22,000 guys up and left, and now what have I got?* Then the Lord speaks again, "Yo, Gideon, you still have *too many* men! Take them down by the brook. The ones that drink the water in a certain way, that's your crew. Get rid of the rest." In the end Gideon is left with 300 men. This is the same Gideon that needed an angel to tell him, "'The Lord is with you, you mighty man of valor!'" (Judges 6:12).

Gideon's reply? "Gideon said to Him, 'O my Lord, if the Lord is with us, why then has all this happened to us?'" (Judges 6:13). Seriously, who hasn't felt like that?

Gideon has one of two thoughts:

1. Lord, are You for real?

    or

2. This is going to be awesome.

In the end, God gets the glory through Gideon. This is a brilliant story.

What about King David? Before he was king, he was hunted like a dog, Saul wanted to kill him out of jealousy. Reading about David is exhilarating; the things he did in and through the Lord, were outstanding.

The one that sticks out to me most was when David went into Saul's heavily guarded and fortified camp at night. If he would have been caught, he would have been killed. He sneaks in and gets very close to Saul while he is sleeping. In fact, David is so close that he cuts a piece of Saul's garment off as proof. *Come on, that has to have the hair on the back of your neck standing up!* David could have killed Saul right then and there and his problems would have been over, but he knew better and said, "I will not stretch out my hand against my lord, for he is the Lord's anointed" (1 Samuel 24:10), and wisely left Saul to God. David's walk before being a king and afterward was extreme (probably more so before), but extreme all the same. For the full story, read 1 Samuel 24:1-22.

David was a man after God's own heart. Was he perfect? Far from it! He made mistakes, and who hasn't? But he loved the Lord. When he realized he had done wrong, he was quick to repent, seek forgiveness, and move forward. David was an amazing man of God and an extreme mover and shaker in God's kingdom plan. Was any of this easy? No! In many of his psalms, David shares his distress and fear. He also attests to the ways God rescued him out of all his troubles, time after time. He never gave up! David walked the extreme walk to the end, trusting his God.

Let's look at Stephen. Does it get more extreme than this? He shows up preaching the gospel in Acts 6:

> And Stephen, full of faith and power, did great wonders and signs among the people (Acts 6:8).

He was framed by the religious leaders and then stoned to death. Before he died, his last words were:

> And they stoned Stephen as he was calling on God and saying, "Lord Jesus, receive my spirit." Then he knelt down and cried out with a loud voice, "Lord, do not charge them with this sin." And when he had said this, he fell asleep (Acts 7:59-60).

You have to have empathy for Stephen, the first martyr. The only thing he was guilty of was being extreme and radical in his faith, preaching Jesus, the cross, and His blood. In Acts 8, he is all but gone, and Saul, who became Paul, was standing right there, condoning and orchestrating the whole thing.

Here is a point to ponder: 2000 years later people are still reading about Stephen, his deeds, and the way he gave his life for the kingdom. You never see books written about people who just sit in the background (or the pew) and watch the church or their work or life happen around them. Look beyond the church for a minute: There's Churchill, Lincoln, Mandela, Patton, and JFK. They all walked an extreme life and made an impact on the world around them. Book after book has been written about their exploits.

Another extreme person was Saul, who became Paul. First he persecuted Christians, putting them to death; then after an encounter with Jesus he was totally transformed. When Saul was sitting in Damascus, blinded and fasting before God, Jesus spoke to a prophet named Ananias about Saul (Paul), saying this,

> But the Lord said to him, "Go, for he is a chosen vessel of Mine to bear My name before Gentiles, kings, and the children of Israel. For I will show him how many things he must suffer for My name's sake" (Acts 9:15-16).

Paul lived probably one of the most extreme lives of all, other than Jesus Himself. He was beaten, stoned (and left for dead), thrown in jail repeatedly, yet still brought glory to the name of Jesus. He had rejected Jesus and everything He was about, persecuting and killing the Christians, and Jesus radically saved him then used him for His glory. Most importantly, Jesus forgave Paul of everything he had done. Paul went on to write most of the New Testament, becoming the single biggest author of that part of the Bible, some of it while in prison.

The most extreme of all was, of course, our King of Kings and Lord of Lords, Yeshua, Messiah, Jesus Christ of Nazareth, Savior, Healer,

Deliverer, Redeemer, Son of the Living God. His was the ultimate walk of them all, now and forever;

Jesus prepared for thirty years for an extreme and an amazing *three-and-a-half-year* ministry. Everywhere He went, there were signs, wonders, and miracles that accompanied the preaching of the kingdom of God, and all who heard Him were healed and set free. I could go on forever about the glorious walk He had. *He walked to the cross to fulfill His destiny, to the glory of the Father.* No one could have stepped in to take His place. Jesus and only Jesus could drink this cup. Though in a minute of weakness, He asked the Father to take this cup from Him, He went on to say, "Father, not My will but Your will be done." Should this not be the cry of our hearts too? Angie and I pray this every morning.

The Twelve asked Jesus to teach them how to pray. He said this:

> When you pray, say: Our Father in heaven, hallowed be Your name. Your kingdom come. Your will be done on earth as it is in heaven. Give us day by day our daily bread. And forgive us our sins, for we also forgive everyone one who is indebted to us. And do not lead us into temptation, but deliver us from the evil one (Luke 11:2-4).

How many of us really pray this? I know there was a time when I said the words, but I was not earnestly seeking the Lord in my heart. I was not quite ready to give everything up to serve the King of Kings. "Your kingdom come, Your will be done on earth as it is in heaven!" Do we really grasp the reality of this statement? I do not think I even understood what it meant. Let's reread a verse from the beginning of this chapter;

> Your eyes saw my substance, being yet unformed. And in Your book they all were written, the days fashioned for me, when as yet there were none of them (Psalm 139:16).

God actually has a book in heaven about each one of us. It was written before the foundation of the world! We are all called to fulfill something we were made to do; we are not called to sit and wait; we are called to use the giftings we have been given for the glory of the Lord. We are to rise up into the fullness of Him who called us. One of the most exciting verses in the Bible is this one:

> Jesus said, "Most assuredly, I say to you, he who believes in Me, the works that I do he will do also; and greater works than these he will do, because I go to My Father. And whatever you ask in My name, that I will do, that the Father may be glorified in the Son. If you ask anything in My name, I will do it" (John 14:12-14).

Who is Jesus speaking to? Every Bible-believing, Bible-speaking, born-again, Spirit-filled believer, that's who! Remember, Jesus has not changed. He is the same yesterday, today, and forever. If He said it, it stands forever.

> God is not a man, that He should lie (Numbers 23:19).

His Word is higher than His name. He will always do what He says He will do.

> For you have magnified Your word above all Your name (Psalm 138:2).

I have given examples about extreme walks in the Bible. About seven years ago, the Lord gave me this word: "An Extreme Walk With Jesus, Don't Settle For Second Best." I truly believe each and every one of us is called to that same extreme walk. What is extreme? That will be different for every person. For one, standing in an elevator and hearing the Lord say, "Smile at that person or say hi"—when that is hard or even frightening for you—can be daunting if you've never done it before or if you're shy by nature. Let's use the word *extreme* for this. For someone else, it may be praying for someone in a wheelchair, sharing your testimony with a complete stranger, standing in a crowd preaching, or going on a mission trip. (Mission trips are awesome adventures, by the way.) Others may be extreme in their giving or called to rescue children from slavery. *An extreme walk fills you with a sense of purpose and direction.* Nothing else will ever make you feel so alive. You will wake every morning excited to meet with the Lord and bask in His glory, waiting upon Him for the day's assignment, opportunity, adventure, or whatever it is. There is always something in Him.

When God told me to go to the nations and speak about "An Extreme Walk With Jesus, Don't Settle For Second Best," the fruit was amazing. I have spoken this word in Australia, Singapore, Malaysia, Indonesia, America, and, just recently, Fiji. The Lord told me, "When you preach about this, end with releasing the gifts that having been lying dormant in My children for such a time as this. Activate the fullness of the call of God upon their lives and then release My glory. Stir the gifts inside My people, and I will do the rest." He has been faithful to do that.

God will be faithful to lift you up and guide you into the call He has on your life, just as he has mine. He has freed you and wants to lead you and bless others through you.

> There is therefore now no condemnation to those who are in Christ Jesus, who do not walk according to the flesh, but according to the Spirit. For the law of the Spirit of life in Christ Jesus has made me free from the law of sin and death (Romans 8:1-2).

I am always amazed at the way Jesus has shown up in my life. My life was always extreme, but when God got ahold of me, it became a glorious extreme, an existence marked by His presence and His joy.

On one trip, I was traveling back from Bundaberg Queensland, Australia after a two-week trip. The Lord had moved and it had been two weeks of non-stop ministry. The glory of God was manifested, gold dust fell, people had visions of heaven, souls were healed, destinies released. Praise the Lord, it was wonderful. On the way back to Melbourne, the door opened to speak in two churches in Wollongong NSW, and again the Lord moved. The next day as we started down the highway, we were about fifteen minutes into the trip back to Melbourne and the Holy Spirit spoke to me and said, "I want you to go to Indonesia." If you knew me, you would know right away that I was thinking, *Yahoo, Yep, Lord, I am in*. I just started smiling, and my friend Joe asked me why. I told him I believed the Holy Spirit had just told me to go to Indonesia. Then I told him that I would need a confirmation. We drove another fifteen or twenty minutes and my cell phone rang. It was Pastor Graham's assistant saying the pastor had asked her to call, asking if I would head up a team to go to Indonesia. Everything in me was already at the airport in my mind, but I told her I would call the pastor and discuss it further with him. I did that, and it was confirmed.

For the rest of our trip, I was on cloud nine (what a dumb saying, cloud nine). Anyway, a couple of hours later we stopped for fuel. My friend and his wife went one way, and when we met back at the car, they were smiling. The Lord had just told them to take the last two weeks off work to come with me on the trip we had just had, and now they turned around and said the Lord had told them to go to Indonesia with me too. It was an amazing trip heading back to Melbourne. Our thoughts were, *Wow! What an amazing God we serve: an excellent road trip and now overseas! Jesus, only Jesus!* I called the pastor's assistant and told her I was in. She said she was booking tickets and I would have to pay by Friday. I had no money but said, "Yep, that will be fine." On Thursday the pastor of the last church where I had preached called and said he had to take off early on Sunday and wanted my bank account details to give a love offering. The love offering paid my airfare and was in my account the following Friday morning.

Pastor Graham contacted Pastor Pantas in Batam Island, Indonesia (an hour-and-twenty-minute boat ride from Singapore) to let him know that a team was coming over. The trip was planned as a twenty-one-day trip which would take us from Batam Island to Median and up into Ache (this is where they train the Taliban). I was very excited and then it came: I had sincere, but sincerely wrong, brothers and sisters in the Lord say, "John, you can't go over there! You have a wife and five boys; it is a very dangerous place to go." First of all, the Holy Spirit told me to go, but second, there is this:

> And they overcame him by the blood of the Lamb and by
> the word of their testimony, and they did not love their
> lives to the death (Revelation 12:11).

I had heard this verse quoted a million times but hardly ever heard the last ten words of this scripture ever mentioned. I had to say to these sincere people, "Look, the Lord told me to go, and to be absent from the body is to be present with the Lord."

> For we walk by faith, not by sight. We are confident, yes,
> well pleased rather to be absent from the body and to be
> present with the Lord (2 Corinthians 5:7-8).

God has given me dreams of the things I am to do for Him, and until those things are accomplished, I know that anywhere the Lord sends me, I will be back. Anyway, the team grew and nine of us went to Indonesia. There was probably only one time when our safety was questionable.

When you trust Abba and you do what He asks, His glory falls. What an amazing trip we had: town to town, city to city. When we left Melbourne, I knew I had one, possibly two, speaking engagements for sure. Some of the team was thinking, *What's up with that?* I tried to explain (having been to Indonesia four to five times by then) that it worked differently there: You land and it is Indo-time. In the end, I spoke one to three times a day for twenty days. I ended up asking Pastor Pantas if one of the other pastors could preach after about thirteen or fourteen days of straight preaching.

When we embarked on this journey, Pastor Pantas had been keen to record the salvations for contact purposes. We had two teams: one team recording salvations and the other recording people being Spirit-filled. It was intense. Team One lost track after a few days, with 363 plus saved; we went to church after church where people had given their lives to the Lord but were not Spirit-filled. Team Two lost track at roughly around 1,000 people who were filled with the Spirit, but there was many more. It was very hard to keep track because everything happened so quickly.

One church stood out. We were praying and believing for miracles when worship started and the glory of God dropped. I was preaching about having an extreme walk with Jesus when the Holy Spirit said, "Open up the altar, it is time to minister." The altar was filled. I heard later that the worship leader looked to the back and saw the angel Gabriel. However, at that point I told my interpreter, "Line them up." The presence of God intensified as I was going down the line; people were getting slain in the Spirit and falling over, and there were people everywhere. Suddenly, I heard screaming. It was so loud that I looked at Pastor Pantas and asked, "What's going on?" He replied, "Do you see the people on the platform? Do you see those two people screaming and crying?" I nodded, and he continued, "Do you see that girl crying and yelling? She has been deaf and mute from birth. Her parents have never seen her talk or hear, and she is now speaking and hearing for the first time in sixteen years!" Then it got even louder as two other young girls' ears popped open! This was incredible. I continued praying for people, and looked at the man in front of me. As I did, the Holy Spirit said, "Release My glory and get out of the way!" So I did. As I prayed and moved to the side, this guy projectile vomited. It was something I had not seen before; it was like on the movies. It just funneled up and out about three to five feet (a little over a yard) as demons came flying out of him and he was set free.

I was brought another young girl who had a withered hand; I prayed for her and nothing seemed to happen. It wasn't until we arrived back to Melbourne when I received a report that her hand, which she had never been able to use, was now usable and getting better (the difference between a miracle and a healing). There were many amazing reports daily. In fact, the whole thing was fun until most of my team up and left me in Indonesia and the eight of them went to Singapore for a three-day shopping spree. Actually, one stayed back for a day or so, but was kind-of encouraged to go to Singapore. The next three days were still awesome, and my trust was in God. I was honored to be asked to speak to the youth on the Saturday night, and then preached Sunday morning at Pastor Pantas's church. After leaving Batam Island, I arrived in Singapore at the hotel to meet the team, so all of us could travel to the airport together. I walked in the back door of the hotel and they were all walking out the front door to go to the airport. If I had been a few minutes later, I would have missed them! (People will be people.) To this day, it was one of the best trips yet, mainly for seeing the Lord move in such glory. I have been to Indonesia many times now. Pastor Pantas is the best. He is such a man of God and a great host. His wife, Momma (everyone calls her Momma), his children, and all the Bible college students who live with him and Momma are beautiful people. On my last trip there, I was being called "Papa John" by the pastor's kids and the students. What an honor to be seen as a father figure (a spiritual father). What a privilege!

There was another thing that was incredible about that trip too. Pastor Pastas introduced me to another pastor from a church who asked me to speak on a radio station the next morning. They were there to get me at five o'clock. I am not a morning person. I get up every morning at around five, have my two cups of coffee, my two-three hours with the Holy Spirit, and *then* I am ready for people. Anyway, here we are driving to the radio station, no coffee and surrounded by chatty people (Perfect). We get to the station and I am given a coffee, praise the Lord. The pastor says we are about to go on air. So I casually ask him three questions:

1. How big is the listening radius?

   The answer is 100 square kilometers, and I think that's a good size.

2. What is your listening audience (How many people listen to this, and I'm thinking maybe 15,000)?

   He says up to 10 million at any given time; I am thinking, *What? Up to 10 million!*

3. My last question is: How long do I speak for? Still pondering up to 10 million listeners.

   He replies roughly two hours. I am thinking *2 hours! One cup of coffee and I'm barely awake!*

The man looked at me and said: "We are on right now." Now, you have to understand something. If you have not yet had the privilege of speaking overseas in a place where you need an interpreter, it is quite the extreme experience. You have to speak, stop, and then let your interpreter relay your message. There are excellent interpreters, and then there are others who really do not understand English much more than the people listening. While you are doing this, you still want to keep the flow of the Spirit. I got about ten minutes in (and it seemed like an hour), while this last part was being translated into Indonesian, I stopped and prayed, "Holy Spirit, I ask in Jesus' name that You would intervene and help here!" (It felt like pulling teeth.) The Holy Spirit took over and the next time I looked at the clock it was an hour and a half later, but it passed like ten minutes. At 1:45, I looked at Pastor Pantas and the other pastor and said, "I believe we are done." That night the church was full of people who came because of what they heard on the radio. All I had done was share my testimony as led by the Holy Spirit, and shared on the love of Jesus and what He did for us and the whole world, gave an altar call, and said the sinner's prayer. I believe there were many who received Jesus as Lord and Savior over the radio. This trip produced salvations, Spirit-filled people, and all kinds of miracles. In the end, the Lord knows the final count and He gets all the glory; we are just available vessels to extend His kingdom.

Are you feeling it yet? *What if?*

What if we all were at the point of saying this? "Lord, I truly surrender all to You! Show me Your glory. Use me, send me, I want to fulfill what is written in my book in heaven. I am tired of chasing the things of the world, I want to be used by You, Daddy, for Your glory. I want everything You have for me, Lord, everything written in my book! Your will be done on earth as it is in heaven. Show me my book, Lord!"

I want to stir every believer's heart for more, more for their lives, more of God in their lives—to challenge every believer to rise up into the fullness of the call of God in their lives, to fulfill their God-given destiny, whatever that is. Throughout this book, there are *what if* sections: lists of thought-provoking, stirring questions (not meant to be condemning, judgmental, or critical). My hope is that they will encourage and empower you. The idea is to bring every believer—no matter where you are—to believe for more. *There is always more in God.*

Extreme living will challenge every believer that the Lord has an extreme walk for *every one* of us. Extreme is anything that takes us out of our comfort zone: "The righteous are as bold as a lion" (Proverbs 28:1). As I said before, extreme can be many things to many people, but this book is to encourage us to all to take stock of where we are with the Lord and say, "Lord, am I truly where You want me to be? If not, show me what I am to be doing for You and show me how to get there."

Twenty years ago the Lord spoke to me and said, "I will cause you to go to many places and you will speak for Me. There will be many who will not have you back. It will not be because of you." Yep, that has happened too. I have gone, done what I was shown to do, seen God move, and it was all over. I had to just move on. Not everyone will understand what you do either. It is before Jesus that we stand or fall. We simply have to be faithful to what He shows us to do, so be encouraged.

Lastly, this book is written for the unsaved—those who have not yet given their lives to the Lord. Jesus is the One and only Savior of the world, and He has a plan for you—a good one. A Christian life is not boring. Jesus has a plan for everyone who will surrender to Him and let Him be the Lord of their life. Angie and I pray that everyone who reads this will come to the end of it with a passion to go deeper in Jesus—deep calling unto deep. This is written for the unsaved, the newly saved, the leaders, and everyone in between: The Lord has so much more for all of us. Go deeper into His glory; the Word says that we go from glory, to glory, to glory. This is never-ending. As we go deeper into Him and see His glory, we should be in a perpetual state of awe and desire for even more of Him and less of us. Angie and I hope this book challenges and blesses each and every reader.

If you truly believe that Jesus died for your sins, ask Him into your life and heart to become your Lord and Savior. He will forgive everything you have ever done! There is nothing He cannot and will not forgive a true, forgiving, and repentant heart—and I mean nothing. Repenting means turning your back on sin and never going back to it; and once forgiven, don't pick it up again! Even though the Devil will try to bring up your past, don't listen. The Devil is a liar, so remind him of his future. If you do not know Jesus, He is waiting for you with open arms. He loves you so much that He died on a cross for you, and the rest of the world. Ask Jesus to come into your life. He will forgive you, wash you in His blood, and set you free. You will never be the same!

Chapter Two: What If? 2.0

W*hat if we could get past ourselves? What if* we could see others—the homeless, the orphan, the widow, the single mothers, the abused, the neglected, the destitute, the hurt, the unsaved, and lost—as Christ sees them? *What if* we could get past the titles, roles, and positions and really serve others? *What if* the church became what it was supposed to be? Instead of being focused inwardly, *what if* we turned that around and became outwardly focused? *What if* people came in, got saved, healed, delivered, set free to the glory of God, and were equipped and released into the world? *What if* churches became more like hospitals and equipping centers instead of waiting rooms? I am not being facetious! When are we going to wake up? *The body of Christ needs to wake up.* We have churches full of wounded and, in some cases, neglected people who have been sitting in the same seat for five, ten, fifteen, and twenty years with the same wounds, scars, and baggage. Some still carry the same unforgiveness they came in with! This should not be.

What if we got back to preaching the gospel in its entirety, and stopped being seeker-friendly? *What if* we stopped worrying about whether or not we will offend this one or that one, and remembered this hard fact: We will all stand before the judgment seat of Christ.

> Therefore, whether we are at home [on earth] or away from home [and with Him], it is our [constant] ambition to be pleasing to Him. For we [believers will be called to account and] must all appear before the judgment seat of Christ, so that each one may be repaid for what has

been done in the body, whether good or bad [that is, each will be held responsible for his actions, purposes, goals, motives—the use or misuse of his time, opportunities and abilities]. Therefore, since we know the fear of the Lord [and understand the importance of obedience and worship], we persuade people [to be reconciled to Him] (2 Corinthians 5:9-11 AMP).

What will we say to Jesus when He asks why we watered down His Word, or why we stopped preaching repentance, the blood, or the cross? What will we say? "Lord, they didn't want to hear it, and I didn't want to offend anyone? Besides, it would affect our tithes and offerings?" Are we going to answer Jesus like that? I don't think so.

Church, we need to wake up! I recently woke up hearing these words: "Tell them I am coming, Tell them I am coming! Tell them I am coming!" The urgency was deafening. First it seemed loud (not sure if it was audible, but very loud just the same) as it was repeated. The deafening part came later as I contemplated it; and now, even a few months later, it still echoes within me. It rings and reverberates in my spirit. This will not go away, so I am telling you now: *Jesus is coming and He is coming soon. What if Jesus came tomorrow?* Would your title matter? Would the size of your church matter? Would how much your tithes and offerings were matter? Would it really matter how excellent your worship team was?

Jesus could return tomorrow, but if He doesn't, *what if we got back to the basics and preached that the kingdom of God is at hand? What if* we preached the gospel in its purity with signs, wonders, and miracles following? We should see people saved, healed, delivered, equipped, and released. The church, like a hospital, should be like a revolving door; the wounded, sick, battered, and beaten people should come in, be healed by the Holy Spirit, set free in the name of Jesus, *equipped (discipled), and sent out to do the work of the ministry*. Yes, I believe it is good to have a covering and a home church, but that should be a place you come and go from, not where you park and wait. Angie and

I recently found a statistic from 2011 that said 54.3 million people die every year. That fluctuates a little each year, but that's not the point. The point is this: How many of these people who die each year go to heaven and enter the kingdom of God?

What if we got past ourselves and focused on the lost and dying people out there? Every year, 54.3 million people die, but what about the billions of lost people who don't know about Jesus?

What if we equipped (discipled) and released the saints (the body) for the work of the ministry? The body has its part to play. It is not supposed to be up to the leadership to do the work. Pastors, we all have to do our part in this Great Commission, but every saint and believer has a part to fulfill as well. *No one is exempt.* We are all called to do something.

Seriously, *what if* instead of singing all our songs that we actually lived them out? For example, we sing these lyrics from Hillsong:

> Jesus at the center of it all,
> Jesus at the center of it all.
> From beginning to the end,
> It will always be, it's always been You, Jesus, Jesus!
>
> Nothing else matters, nothing in this world will do;
> Jesus, You're the center; everything revolves around You!
> Jesus, You, at the center of it all, the center of it all.
>
> Jesus, be the center of my life!
> Jesus, be the center of my life!
> From beginning to the end
> It will always be, it's always been You, Jesus! Jesus![1]

1. Israel Houghton, Micah Massey, and Adam Ranney, writers, "Jesus at the Center," recorded February 2012, in Jesus at the Center, Israel Houghton & New Breed, Integrity / Columbia, 2012, CD. Used by permission of Copycare Pacific Pty Ltd.

I love this song; we listen to it all the time, but we sing, "Jesus at the center of it all, Jesus, You're the center, and everything revolves around You, oh, Jesus, be the center of my life!" on a Sunday. For the most part, I believe most people sing it with heartfelt sincerity, wanting that exact thing. But Monday comes and everything we sang, felt, and believed is all but gone; the reality of life comes flooding back with its jobs, school, kids, hobbies, entertainments, responsibilities, addictions, whatever—and they consume our world until Sunday rolls around again. Then we are back in His house and the praise and worship takes us back to that place of basking in His presence and feeling His glory. There we are in an endless cycle of wanting Him more, hoping, praying, believing, but then making promises we know we can't or won't keep. Then bam, church ends and you start to dread Monday—and it begins all over again. For some, addictions kick in and it was like church was a figment of their imagination: crazy but real. Been there, done that, bought the T-shirt! You know what Jesus offers is right, but never seem to be able to get there; and if you ever do, it is short-lived. Does it mean we don't believe or don't want to be set free? No.

What if you could be set free—I mean really set free? Is there a difference? Absolutely! I have personal experience in this area. Having used drugs for a couple of decades (daily), I often tried to quit. I would have a go for some time, and even have some success. However, it wasn't long before something would happen (tough time with friends, family issues, a bad day, or just the spirit of addiction) and there I was—back on the pipe or whatever it was.

> Jesus answered them, "Most assuredly, I say to you, whoever commits sin is a slave of sin. And a slave does not abide in the house forever, but a son abides forever. Therefore if the Son makes you free, you shall be free indeed" (John 8:34-36).

Wow! Let's unpack that for a minute. This has blown me away. You know how you take things from the Bible and they become a "reality scripture" for you? You have to take the time to read the surrounding scriptures too. This helps us see the context of the idea in the verse, and gives us the perspective behind what is being said. Then it cannot be taken out of proportion, out of context, or wrongly applied to manipulate a situation. This verse is now a reality in my life because I can say that I am free indeed. I no longer have a drug problem. I no longer struggle with sins that held me captive in my past. So let's go back a bit and start at verse 34 to get the context.

> "Most assuredly, I say to you, whoever commits sin is a slave of sin" (John 8:34).

Right there we have to stop. The phrase, *most assuredly* should be enough to slam on the brakes: Jesus is *warning us*! He is saying, "Hey there, you listen up, I am telling you something here, so *pay attention*! Are you listening? "I say to you, whoever commits sin is a slave of sin!" And who was He speaking to? Jesus was talking to *believers*. Let's go back a little more so you can see that:

> "Then Jesus said to those Jews who believed Him, 'If you abide in My word, you are My disciples indeed. And you shall know the truth, and the truth shall make you free'" (John 8:31-32).

These are Jesus' words, not mine. Too many of us are caught up in things that keep us from walking in the freedom of Christ.

> "And a slave does not abide in the house forever, but a son abides forever" (John 8:35).

There are far too many people in the house of God today who are trapped in sin and enslaved to it. One of my pet peeves is that we see people blatantly in sin or know of their sin and we do nothing. You even hear of people being hurt because of this. Some years back a guy wanted to start a church so he was released as a pastor and opened his own church. However, reports kept coming back of sexual misconduct (and not just once), as well as lying and various other incidents. And yet, when it was brought up, those responsible for overseeing this pastor said, "We must have grace." Grace? I did not agree, and I felt the "spirit of slap" coming upon me. What kind of "grace" was that? Grace in this situation would have been to reprimand that pastor and remove him (for good or a season, dependent upon the Holy Spirit's direction). It was obvious that there were unresolved issues with this pastor that have still not been dealt with! This needs to be taken care of properly before more people in the church are damaged as a result. Grace is not a license to sin—and definitely not by anyone in leadership!

> My brethren, let not many of you become teachers, knowing
> that we shall receive a stricter judgment (James 3:1).

I believe we need great grace, but we must not condone sin in any way, shape, or form. Sin should be addressed in love to bring a person to the place where sonship is so evident that sin is a thing of the past, *as a son abides in the house forever.* Don't get me wrong: we definitely need to show grace toward the newly-saved as they are being discipled, but that same kind of grace should not be necessary for someone who is supposedly mature in Christ. We are called to *equip the saints for the work of the ministry* and see believers healed, delivered, and set free from the world and the things of the world, so we can stand and share how the Son has made us free indeed.

What if we were all free?

> Therefore if the Son makes you free, you shall be free
> indeed (John 8:36).

The deeper I go with the Lord, the more I truly appreciate what He has done for me. I have never been so free! What an awesome God we serve! Does it get any better than this? The answer to that is yes, absolutely yes. It just gets better and better! As we grow closer to Jesus, we get freer still; and more and more opens up to us. It is hard to imagine sometimes that it can get better, but it can.

There is absolutely nothing greater than serving the Lord with all your heart, soul, and mind, believing that God, the Creator of the heavens and earth, has something awesome for each and every one. He never intended that we would get saved and do nothing. No, each and every one is called to something. Abba is looking for those who love Him to say, "Daddy, pick me! Send me! Use me! Here I am, Lord." Take a moment now and pray this:

> *Lord, I say yes to Your perfect plan, the plan written in my book, before I was formed in my mother's womb. I say yes!*

What if we could all walk a sinless life? In Romans, it says:

> For all have sinned and fall short of the glory of God (Romans 3:23).

Yep, that's right: every one of us. There was, and is, only One who was sinless—Jesus Christ of Nazareth. Does God condemn us for this? Does He want to shame us? No, Romans also says this:

> There is therefore now no condemnation to those who are in Christ Jesus, who do not walk according to the flesh, but according to the Spirit. For the law of the Spirit of life in Christ Jesus has made me free from the law of sin and death (Romans 8:1-2).

If we truly want to walk in the glory that will be poured out on the nations for this end-time harvest, we need to go up to the next level (perhaps levels). We need to grow up and mature. No more milk; it is time for meat! I am a true carnivore. I love meat. Ain't nothing better than a two-inch thick T-bone or ribs (and barbecued if I can get them.) However, I love the meat of the Word even more. Everyone makes mistakes (and I mean everyone) and yes, His grace is sufficient, but we do not remain in our sin.

> And He said to me, "My grace is sufficient for you, for My strength is made perfect in weakness" (2 Corinthians 12:9).

Paul was writing this about himself and an affliction he had, but it still applies to us in our weakness. We are made strong in Him. However, do we use this same grace as an excuse for sin? I, like Paul say, no. Paul went on to say this:

> For sin shall not have dominion over you, for you are not
> under law but under grace (Romans 6:14).

God is about to clean house. The accepted sin in the church today will no longer be tolerated in the future. We are going to see the time of Ananias and Sapphira reappear. The Lord is about to reap one of the greatest harvests ever seen, according to prophecies from Bob Jones and many others: one billion souls! Here's the problem as I see it: The church is not prepared for a great harvest. Instead of being ready, without stain or wrinkle, the church is a splintered mess. In her current state, it is necessary for a complete overhaul. What has been done in the dark will now be exposed to the light.

> For there is nothing hidden which will not be revealed,
> nor has anything been kept secret but that it should come
> to light (Mark 4:22).

The Lord has extended His grace for a long time, and now He is going to expose all: all the corruption, ungodly agendas, perversion, embezzlement, and the like. Daddy is not going to send dirty people (unsaved) into a dirty church. No, He is going to clean His house, so that when the lost come in and become found, they will be truly cleansed and released into a healthy house with a strong, clean foundation. Only then can these new souls be equipped, trained, and then released, as it was always supposed to be in Ephesians 4:11-12.

I pray for the day when a pastor can see the potential in another and not be threatened by that person, but help them instead. May pastors see the God-given gifts and calling and work to equip that person for the work of the ministry, not hold them back or crush the call out of them. As I write this, I must say that I have seen people held down and held back by leaders, and it grieves the Lord. Are we not to use Jesus as our example?

> Then Jesus answered and said to them, "Most assuredly, I say to you, the Son can do nothing of Himself, but what He sees the Father do; for whatever He does, the Son also does in like manner" (John 5:19).

And there it is again, *Most assuredly. Listen!* He is trying to get our attention again.

So, ministers of the gospel, Jesus only did what the Father did, and we are to imitate Christ. Why do we fear when someone comes to the church, and you and everyone around you can see the call of God on them? Should we not embrace them and protect, nurture, and equip them? And then give them opportunities and raise them into maturity, so they can walk out their destinies? (I was blessed to be with Pastor Graham. He gave me opportunities in Australia and internationally!) God opens doors, but He uses His leaders. We should not fear these people for trying to walk in what they were called to do or because they are different or because they have a greater calling than we do. Did Jesus fear this? Was Jesus worried that one of His disciples would outpreach Him? Or do greater miracles? Or be preferred by the crowds? Nope! On the contrary, He said:

> Most assuredly, I say to you, he who believes Me, the works that I do he will do also; and greater works than these will he do, because I go to My Father. And whatever you ask in My name, that I will do, that the Father may be glorified in the Son. If you ask anything in My name, I will do it (John 14:12-14).

There is that "most assuredly" again! When Jesus uses this phrase, He is really trying to get a point across. I would have been speechless. Jesus is not saying, "Hey, maybe you will do okay at this gig." He is saying, "Get this: If you believe in Me, (and that means *anyone* who believes) the works I do, *you* will also do! But hang on, there's more!

He says you will do even *greater works* than these! Why? Because Jesus says, "I go to My Father." Come on! Jesus is telling us we are to *do greater works than Him*! That doesn't sound right. Yep, that is what it says: Jesus wants us to *excel* to greater things than He did. Shouldn't we want the same for those Daddy gives us to mentor and equip? Should we not become spiritual fathers, mothers, mentors, and teachers to others and truly hope and believe they can rise up and exceed anything we have ever done for His glory? Let's explore why Jesus said this.

If we eagerly take on the men and women the Lord gives us with a heart attitude of raising them up into the *fullness* of their God-given destiny, the Father will be glorified in the Son. Anything we do in the name of Jesus glorifies the Father. Today more than ever, we need spiritual fathers and mothers who are moved beyond compassion to see their spiritual children overtake them by light years. We need people who would be exhilarated by that process. How glorious would that be!

In the last chapter, I mentioned I was witnessing to an atheist. Nick was an awesome guy, but he struggled with the "whole church thing" (his words). He told me he saw Christians as hypocritical. As he went on, I thought, *that's valid!* I explained that Christianity was not supposed to be that way. He was adamant that Christians said one thing and did another: They preached Jesus, yet went to the same pubs, nightclubs, and parties as everyone else. They were having sex, committing adultery, drinking, doing drugs, and so on. They did the same things he did, yet he heard them tell him he needed Jesus. So he said to me, "Why do I need Jesus, God, or church if they do the exact same things I do?" (Now Nick does not do drugs or the other things on that list, but he was trying to make a point about what he saw). Unfortunately, he was not wrong in his evaluation of the church as a whole. We are supposed to be *in* the world, *but not part* of the world. We should stand out as different—and this is why I believe God is about to clean house. It has already started, but will intensify before the great outpouring of His glory.

> For the time has come for judgment to begin at the house of God (1 Peter 4:17).

In my twenty-five years of being Spirit-filled and having had the privilege to attend many different churches (I never church-hopped, but I did move many times), I have seen some pretty amazing things done in the name of Jesus. We don't have time to play church anymore; It is time to become the body of Christ without spot or wrinkle because that is what Jesus is coming back for.

What if we could get past envy, pride, greed, self-ambition, selfish motives and agendas, gossip, slander, racism, bigotry, chauvinism, division, denominationalism, and all that, and become the true body of Christ, being in one accord, in unity of the Spirit with one focus and one agenda—Jesus' agenda?

The Great Commission is:

> And Jesus came and spoke to them, saying, "All authority has been given to Me in heaven and on earth. Go therefore and make disciples of all the nations, baptizing them in the name of the Father and of the Son and of the Holy Spirit, teaching them to observe all things that I have commanded you; and lo, I am with you always, even to the end of the age." Amen (Matthew 28:18-20).

Again, this is not a, "Hey man, if you have the time kinda thing." Jesus commissioned *all of us* to go into the world, our world—whatever that looks like. In the early church days after Jesus went to sit at the right hand of Abba, His Father, those who followed Him were called Christians. They were not divided into Baptists, Catholics, Eastern Orthodox, Anglicans, Protestants, and Pentecostals. Today when I searched "Christian denominations" on the Internet, it said there are 43,000 different Christian denominations. By 2025, there will be roughly 55,000, and each will have their own beliefs and doctrinal ideology. Crazy, right?

So *what if* we could all get on the same page as the Master? *What if* we put our petty differences aside and went and made "disciples of all the nations," fulfilling our mandate to the Lord? *What if* we were focused on teaching them to observe what Christ has commanded us? That would require that we walk that way first. The up side to this is His promise that if we do what He is asking, He will be with us. He said, "And lo, I am with you always, even to the end of the age. Amen." Again amen, "so be it."

Can you imagine what it would be like if all Christians came together, put aside their religious traditions, laid down every offense and criticism, and took up their cross and followed Jesus? What a glorious day that would be! We must stop striving to have what the world has and do the work of the ministry.

What if we put Jesus first in all that we do?

What if we asked Jesus what He wanted us to do with our lives? And then did it!

I heard a Christian speaker once who talked about the difference between a job, a career, and a vocation. Here are the definitions:

Job: A paid position of regular employment.[2]

Career: An occupation undertaken for a significant period of a person's life and with opportunities for progress.[3]

Vocation: A vocation is an occupation to which a person is specially drawn or for which she/he is suited, trained, or qualified. Though now often used in non-religious contexts, the meaning of the term originated in Christianity.[4]

2. "Job | Definition of Job in English by Oxford Dictionaries," Oxford Dictionaries | English, accessed February 24, 2019, https://en.oxforddictionaries.com/definition/job.

3. "Career | Definition of Career in English by Oxford Dictionaries," Oxford Dictionaries | English, accessed February 24, 2019, https://en.oxforddictionaries.com/definition/career.

4. "Vocation," Wikipedia, December 14, 2018, accessed February 25, 2019, https://en.wikipedia.org/wiki/Vocation.

For roughly twenty years, I had a career in real estate. Although it paid the bills, it wasn't fulfilling. It had its highs and lows as that industry does; but the closer I grew to the Lord, the harder it was to do it. After I learned that the meaning of *vocation* referred to something to which one should be specially drawn, or uniquely suited or qualified, I really started seeking the Lord about my vocation *in Him*. What was I to be doing for Him?

I began to pray and seek God about this in a fresh way. At two o'clock in the morning one day, I woke up hearing, "I commission you to go to the nations! Go to the nations and preach! Save My people! Go now!" Those words rocked my world! Just try and go back to sleep after that! Clearly full-time ministry was my vocation. I had waited more than ten years to hear that. I had tastes of it every now and again; but with His assurance, I could now step into it full-time to the glory of the Lord.

I am not suggesting that everyone should be in full-time ministry. *If you have a job or career and you know God is in it, then that is where you are supposed to be.* However, if you are doing something you do not enjoy, or even worse, hate, then you need to seek the Lord about why you are there. He may have a purpose behind it; but if He does not, ask Him to show you what your vocation in Him should be.

However, I digress. Let's get back to a *what if.*

What if we could be as bold as lions in doing what we were called to do? We could share our faith and see people saved and delivered. In turn, they would be out doing the same thing. I think if we looked at the whole situation from a different perspective and really saw the situation for what it is, it would blow us all away.

God the Father does not need our help. He could use His angels or just speak and it would be done. However, He has chosen to use us (humans) for His glory because He loves us all. He doesn't have favorites. (Okay, maybe the Israelites have been pretty special, but as a whole, God loves us all equally.)

What if we got so hungry for the Lord that the things of the world became truly dim? *What if* those things were irrelevant to us? *What if* we got so kingdom-focused and kingdom-minded that we were walking completely devoted, righteous lives?

> But seek first the kingdom of God and His righteousness,
> and all these things shall be added to you (Matthew 6:33).

If we stop chasing the things of the world and chase God and His righteousness instead, He will give us all these things anyway. We serve an awesome God. When He has our hearts, He has everything. When we ask of Him, He will give us what we ask for. Just through writing this book, I am falling into a deeper love for the One who set me free! Thank You, Jesus. It makes me think of the true goodness of Abba; what an awesome, amazing, incredible, unstoppable, omnipotent, omnipresent Father He is! He is able to turn every *what if* into "It is done!" and "It is good!"

What if you were to look at where you are at and say, "Lord, there has to be more"?

What if you looked at your life and said, "Lord, I want an extreme walk with You. I do not want to settle for second best"?

I have had some awesome adventures in Jesus in my life, but I still cry out for this all the time. Most days I say, "Holy Spirit, I know there is more. I want to walk in the fullness of the call upon my life. I do not want to miss anything You have for me. Jesus, I want to glorify Your name into the nations. Abba, I want all of You! I am so hungry for You. I love You, Lord. Use me, send me. Lord, I will go wherever You send me. I will say whatever You tell me to say. I will do whatever You tell me to do. Pick me, Lord!" This is where I am in my heart. I simply cannot sit by and watch people go to hell and do nothing. I have a responsibility to them. My heart burns within me. It is written:

> For everyone to whom much is given, from him much
> will be required (Luke 12:48).

Man, does this apply to me! I have been forgiven of a great deal. I have done many awful things over the course of my life and I am truly grateful I found Jesus. Actually, I think He found me. I wasn't looking for Him. He was looking for me! How blessed and fortunate I am!

What if I could convince you that there is an extreme walk for you?

What if I could get you to believe that walking on the edge is not only fun, but actually exhilarating and wonderful?

What if I could stir your heart to believe for more?

> Therefore I remind you to stir up the gift of God which is in you through the laying on of my hands. For God has not given us a spirit of fear, but of power and of love and of a sound mind (2 Timothy 1:6-7).

The word *activate* is synonymous with the words *stir up.* When I am preaching and nearing the end of my message, the Lord has me release the gifts that are sitting dormant in people and then activate (or stir up) the call of God upon their lives through the Holy Spirit. (We can do nothing without the Holy Spirit.) God does this so people will rise up into the fullness of their callings and potential, whatever that may be.

What if this is happening to you right now? Your spirit is being stirred, and what you are reading is impacting you right where you sit. Your heart is crying out: "Yes, there has to be more."

If this is the case, I ask you to pray this out loud:

> *Father, I come before You in Jesus' name, and I ask You, Daddy, to show me who I am in You, to show me the fullness of the call upon my life. Abba, I want to fulfill everything written in my book, the book that was written before the foundation of the world for me. All my days were written before there were any. Lord, I want to walk an extreme walk with You, no matter what it looks like. I do not want to settle for second best. Holy Spirit, I ask that You release every gift that has been lying dormant in me for such a time as this; activate the fullness of the call of God upon my life and release Your glory into my*

life now in Jesus' name. I seal this in the name and blood of Jesus. Jesus, it is written in John 14:14 that if I ask anything in Your name, You will do it, so I believe and receive this now. Thank You, Jesus. Amen.

When I was in Indonesia on one of my trips, we went to an island which I can't pronounce, to a church in the middle of a jungle. There were no cars or trucks there, so we had to travel on the back of mopeds. It was great in the daytime and extremely dangerous at night because we had to use paths through a jungle that was also inhabited by tigers and other creatures. One night we had a ferocious storm. As we went through the jungle, it rained so hard that we could not even see the headlights in front of us. The downpour was extreme and lightning flashed above our heads and lit up the path for a split second, we could not see anything. Earlier that night as I was ministering, the Holy Spirit stopped me and told me to ask the pastors to come up and release God's glory over them. Roughly a third of the church came to the front, and I (through the Holy Spirit) prophesied over each one of them. It was truly amazing to find that all these leaders had traveled from so many islands to get there to receive a touch from the Lord in the middle of this jungle. They were truly hungry servants of God. Through that, God showed me that no matter where you are in the Lord, there is always more. We only need a receptive and pure heart.

I pray that this truth penetrates the hearts of those reading: that each and every heart will be stirred to believe there is more, so much more. Pray with me.

Lord, we ask that every heart would cry out for a deeper walk with You. Holy Spirit, release Your glory over us now in the name of Jesus. Deep calling unto deep, release the fullness of the call of God upon us, Lord. Give each and every one of us dreams, visions, and revelation of the greater things to which You have called us to. Show us Your glory, Lord, as You showed Moses, Joseph, Daniel, and so many more. Burn into us our destinies and the desire to fulfill everything written in our books in heaven, that we would glorify You, Lord, in all that we do. Thank You, Lord! We pray this in Jesus' name, believing for each and every person reading this right now. May we be stirred by You, Holy Spirit, and never be the same again. Amen.

This chapter is meant to be thought-provoking, *What if we all desired to fulfill our destinies? What if we stepped out of our comfort zones and walked in the supernatural* to the glory of the Lord? Let's do that. Let's say, "Yes, Lord, pick me, I am all in! I want an extreme walk with You, Lord!"

Angie and I have come to that place. Unless it is extreme, we would rather go home to be with the Father. Extreme living is different for each and every one of us; but when we surrender everything to Jesus and put Him first—before everything else—in a real relationship with Him, our lives become extreme. When this occurs, it is no longer us at the helm. It is Jesus. When the Spirit rules, miracles happen. Are you ready for miracles?

Chapter Three: Joseph

I think everybody can relate to someone in the Bible. I can relate to a few people. I feel a kinship with Moses, Paul, and Joseph too. Let's start with Joseph.

Joseph's story is amazing. Here's a kid who has these dreams when he is seventeen. Let's try to picture this for what it is. He has two dreams, and here is the first one:

> Now Jacob dwelt in the land where his father was a stranger, in the land of Canaan. This is the history of Jacob. Joseph, being seventeen years old, was feeding the flock with his brothers. And the lad was with the sons of Bilhah and the sons of Zilpah, his father's wives; and Joseph brought a bad report of them to his father. Now Israel loved Joseph more than all his children, because he was the son of his old age. Also he made him a tunic of many colors. But when his brothers saw that their father loved him more than all his brothers, they hated him and could not speak peaceably to him. Now Joseph had a dream, and he told it to his brothers; and they hated him even more. So he said to them, "Please hear this dream which I have dreamed: There we were, binding sheaves in the field. Then behold, my sheaf arose and also stood upright; and indeed your sheaves stood all around and bowed down to my sheaf." And his brothers said to him, "Shall you indeed reign over us? Or shall you indeed have

dominion over us?" So they hated him even more for his dreams and for his words (Genesis 37:1-8).

Does this happen today? Seriously, Joseph had this wildly amazing dream and thought, *Hey man, I gotta share this with someone. I know, I will share it with my family. They will believe with me.* Joseph was ecstatic about his dream because he knew it was a true God-dream. What else could he do? This was so big that he just couldn't help but share it. He may have innocently thought his family would have been jumping up and down for joy with him. After all, this was part of God's plan. I would have loved to be there watching it unfold: Joseph would have been sharing his dream with his brothers and waiting for them to say: "Hey, man, that is awesome! We've got your back!" But instead "they hated him even more for his dreams and for his words." I'm sure Joseph was thinking, *Wow, guys, this is going to be wonderful and it is going to be for all of us.* Instead, he experienced total rejection. Then he had the second dream;

> Then he dreamed still another dream and told it to his brothers, and said, "Look, I have dreamed another dream. And this time, the sun, the moon, and the eleven stars bowed down to me." So he told it to his father and his brothers; and his father rebuked him and said to him, "What is this dream that you have dreamed? Shall your mother and I and your brothers indeed come to bow down to the earth before you?" And his brothers envied him, but his father kept the matter in mind (Genesis 37:9-11).

Yep, Joseph felt the need to share that second dream too. I don't know why. Maybe he was thinking the second would add credence to the first. As I was writing this I thought, *Man, Joseph needed some sort of how-to successfully-cast-your-vision manual right about then. It sure would have been helpful!* I chuckled and thought, *Well, that is what the Bible is, isn't it? We need an Idiot's Guide to the Bible; they have guides written for everything else.* In Joseph's case, this all happened by design. All these things had been written in his book; and without all these events, God couldn't show His hand in the life of the Israelites. His plan was surprising, complex, and written in Joseph's book.

Let's jump ahead thousands of years and see how this fits in today. In the natural realm, Joseph's brothers would have looked at him and thought, *Look at this guy! Who does he think he is? Listen to the pride and arrogance that comes out of his mouth! He thinks he is better than everyone else. He thinks his calling is better than ours!* (You get the picture. This still happens in the church today when someone gossips about another.) Joseph was not being prideful nor arrogant. He knew his God, and he knew His voice. He knew his destiny, and he knew his authority; and in the end, the truth of his dreams became apparent to all the naysayers, his father included. When that time came, Joseph did not say, "I told you so"; he extended grace and mercy to them. He invited them back into his life, forgave them, and said, "You did nothing wrong! The Lord used all this for His good" (paraphrased).

> And we know that all things work together for good to those who love God, to those who are called according to His purpose (Romans 8:28).

There is so much to take from the story of Joseph, but right now I want to share some of what I have learned the hard way. I have learned that not everyone will be happy for you when you share your dreams or when they hear a prophecy over your life. In your presence, they may seem genuinely happy for you, but behind your back, they are not. Instead of support, they will knife you in the back—and some of them will be your closest friends.

I was at a conference about seven or so years ago in Melbourne, Australia. I was picked out of a crowd by a speaker (a well-known apostle), and he began prophesying over me by saying that the Lord had just shown him all the wounds and scars in my back, and what I had suffered for the Lord. This in itself would have been amazing, but it was not the first time. It was actually the second or third time that a minister of the gospel stopped what they were doing, picked me out of a crowd, and spoke about that very thing over my life; and each time it was almost word for word.

He went on to prophesy the same thing over my life that has been prophesied for twenty-five years or so: that I was to reap a huge harvest of souls and that millions and hundreds of millions of dollars would go through my hands for the kingdom's sake. This has been an ongoing prophecy and it is always the same. It has never changed and also runs concurrently with all the dreams He has given me for the last thirty-two years. Now here's the kicker: People either hate you for those dreams and the calling on your life, or they latch on to them, believing for the millions. No one was willing to walk the walk or pay the price that it has taken to get to where I am at today (and similarly, where Joseph had to go). I am still waiting on the Lord for the millions and hundreds of millions for the kingdom's sake, and other parts of those dreams (which I will share later). Abba has spoken through His Holy Spirit, and I know that I know this is all to come. He said it. I believe and receive it.

> For assuredly, I say to you, whoever says to this mountain, "Be removed and be cast into the sea," and does not doubt in his heart, but believes that those things he says will be done, he will have whatever he says. Therefore I say to you, whatever things you ask when you pray, believe that you receive them, and you will have them (Mark 11:23-24).

The bigger issue is that the Lord spoke to me. I heard it, and later the same words have been spoken to me by prophets, apostles, pastors, evangelists, and a teacher too. That word has been confirmed many times. If it were just me, maybe someone could say, "Whoa, no, you're missing it!" Or even, "Perhaps that's just your idea and not God's calling!" But the Bible says this:

> By the mouth of two or three witnesses every word shall be established (2 Corinthians 13:1).

God confirms His direction for people through the five-fold ministries. That's His plan. Over the years, I have had people who have come into my life with their own agenda. Their motivation has been to get where they wanted to go, but they have tried to do that with me because of that prophetic word in my life, using it to their own ends. Seeing this has made my heart sad. I want to join with those serving God for His glory; but as in Joseph's time, people react differently to the way God's plan is intended to work out. Joseph's brothers wanted to whack him; instead they sold him into slavery. They did not see the gift or the call on Joseph's life. All they saw was arrogance and pride (haven't I heard that before), and did not recognize the authority and power that had been placed upon Joseph when he believed that what he received was from God. Some have wondered, "Did he really know all that when he was only seventeen?" Yes, he did. He knew the Lord. We know this from this portion of Genesis 39:

> Now Joseph had been taken down to Egypt. And Potiphar, an officer of Pharaoh, captain of the guard, an Egyptian, bought him from the Ishmaelites who had taken him down there. The Lord was with Joseph, and he was a successful man; and he was in the house of his master the Egyptian. And his master saw that the Lord was with him and that the Lord made all he did to prosper in his hand. So Joseph found favor in his sight, and served him. Then he made him overseer of his house, and all that he had he put under his authority. So it was, from the time that he had made him overseer of his house and all that he had, that the Lord blessed the Egyptian's house for Joseph's sake; and the blessing of the Lord was on all that he had in the house and in the field. Thus he left all that he had in Joseph's hand, and he did not know what he had except for the bread which he ate. Now Joseph was handsome in form and appearance. And it came to pass after these things that his master's wife cast longing eyes on Joseph, and she said, "Lie with

me." But he refused and said to his master's wife, "Look, my master does not know what is with me in the house, and he has committed all that he has to my hand. There is no one greater in this house than I, nor has he kept back anything from me but you, because you are his wife. How then can I do this great wickedness, and sin against God?" (Genesis 39:1-9).

We have to look at the reality of Joseph's life: Sold into slavery, he knew who he was in the Lord. He did not allow himself to be subject to other people's thoughts or agendas and he would not sin, and certainly not against God. What a guy! It's oddly funny, but the same people who sold him down the river and were judging him were the guilty ones. What is the lesson here so far? *When the Lord shows you something, guard it with your heart.* Really guard it; do not share it with just anyone. There are two reasons for this:

1. Not everyone will be happy for you. (Jealousy, envy and all sorts of malice could arise as a result.)

2. If you are not understood, words will be spoken against you and your dream. These can affect you and where you are going (Isaiah 54:17).

I would like to share an example of this first point. It began in the preparation for one of my trips to Indonesia. We were building a team and getting together weekly to pray and prepare. While we were having dinner one day, a pastor who was one of the team members looked at me and said, "You know, John, I am going to struggle in submitting to you because you have only just been released as a pastor, and I have been a pastor for some years." I laughed and thought, *That is an odd thing to say.* Well, let me tell you this: If anyone ever says anything like that to you, *stop what you are doing and seek the Lord!* Hindsight is a good teacher. Now that it is all over, I realize that he was really saying this: "I have been a pastor longer and I should be in charge, not you." Knowing what I know now, I should have said, "Maybe this trip is not for you." The Lord told me to go. He didn't ask me *to join* a team. After my many overseas trips as a team member, I was *to lead* this one. Of that, I was sure.

Within a few days of our arrival in Indonesia, it started. Wow, and did it start! Have you heard the old saying: "When in Rome, do as the Romans do?" Well, in Indonesia it is "Indo Time"! When the pastor says, "John, I will pick you up tomorrow morning at ten," you are ready at nine (just in case) and will be picked up by eleven, or in the worse-case scenario: lunchtime. It's strange but fun all at the same time. Well, this pastor (It was his first time to Indonesia) started saying that I should demand that the Indonesian pastor be told to be on time. He then started telling the rest of the team that I should not be leading the team. He said I was incapable. He did everything he could to make me look bad. Next, he talked the team into abandoning me in Indonesia, and going to Singapore on a shopping spree (where he could be the one in charge) for the last three days. But when God is in control of things, He has a way of sorting it all out. The Indonesian pastor and I had lunch on my last day. He spoke for a while and then told me that the Lord had shown him the condition of this pastor's heart, and that this was the reason he had not wanted him to preach on the trip. Later, the pastor sent a report back to my church, outlining everything that had happened. When I got back, I shared all that God had done, giving God the glory for the trip. I did not mention any problems with anyone. In my eyes, the good report was the real story on our trip, and it was awesome: Hundreds or more saved, more than a thousand spirit-filled! That was praiseworthy.

As the Lord lifts you up, do not expect everyone to be happy for you. Be careful of what you share and with whom you share it. Pastor Graham used to say this to me: "John, share with people who are at your level or higher. Stay away from the Dream Crushers and the Dream Killers. Only share with people who can believe with you and for you." Joseph's brothers envied him; they were killers and crushers.

Pastor Graham is my spiritual father. He believes with me and for me. One day we were having lunch, and he said to me, "I have to be honest with you, John. Many times you have told me the things the Lord has shown you. I have listened and I went before the Lord and asked

Him, 'Lord, You know everything John has said You have told him. Is this of You or has he missed it, big time?'" Pastor Graham went on to say that the Lord spoke to him and confirmed that the things I had said and seen were from God.

Just like Joseph's father, after I shared my dreams and the words I heard from God with Pastor Graham, he "kept the matter *in mind.*" He went to the Lord about things I had shared with him over the years, pondering whether or not I was hearing from God or out in left field. When he told me this, I started laughing. I thought, *Man, you have prophesied over me so many times and heard many guest speakers prophesy the same things in front of you!* But then he took the time to take it to the Lord and wait on Him about it for me. How important it is to share with only those who can believe for you and with you! I am thankful that Pastor Graham stands and believes with me. Now that I am older, when the Lord speaks, I am able to keep it to myself, except for my wife. I share everything with Angie. Even so, we wait for the Lord to confirm things through people—people who have no idea of what we are waiting for.

In the past, I did not share things because I thought I was better than anyone, or in a prideful or arrogant way. However, in my exuberance and zeal, I shared my dreams and prophecies with others, trying to get everyone to rise to the fullness of the call of God upon their lives, as a way of stirring the gifts. (It was not always taken that way.) Yet the truth is (and I believe it wholeheartedly) that everyone has a God-given call:

For many are called, but few are chosen (Matthew 22:14).

God has callings for everyone: for those who give their lives to the Lord, the ones who truly ask Jesus to become King of Kings and Lord of Lords in their lives. Psalm 139 doesn't say there is a book written for some; that scripture is for all mankind but that promise is only found in Him. Many are called, but few are chosen, but I actually think all are called.

> The Lord is not slack concerning *His promise*, as some count slackness, but is longsuffering toward us, not willing that *any* should perish but that *all* should come to repentance (2 Peter 3:9, emphasis mine).

As far as *chosen*, I think that refers to our choice. We decide if we are going to surrender all to Him or if that is just something we sing about on Sunday morning. We can even deny the call completely. To walk an extreme life, we have to let the world go and let God have His way.

Let's move on to lesson two. Here is Joseph: He is a slave but the blessing of God is all over him. Potiphar's promiscuous wife lies about him, making false accusations against him (Wow, déjà vu for me there!), and then in the natural, Potiphar demotes him and puts him in prison. Isn't this just great? Here is a guy who had two dreams about people bowing down to him, and now he is in a dungeon. Has this ever happened to you? You receive a mind-blowing prophecy (that you did not even ask for!) and now you are further away than when you started? In the natural realm, Joseph had to be thinking, *God, come on, already! This is not what You showed me. This is not what You called me to at all! I saw it; I could breathe it; it was real; it was tangible! Prison? Really?* But the Lord's hand was upon Joseph;

> Then Joseph's master took him and put him into the prison, a place where the king's prisoners were confined. And he was there in the prison. But the Lord was with Joseph and showed him mercy, and He gave him favor in the sight of the keeper of the prison. And the keeper of the prison committed to Joseph's hand all the prisoners who were in the prison; whatever they did there, it was his doing. The keeper of the prison did not look into anything that was under Joseph's authority, because the Lord was with him; and whatever he did, the Lord made it prosper (Genesis 39:20-23).

This is amazing! Even in the natural, prison seemed worse than his last place, but the Lord was with him again. We only ever hear that he did everything unto God; but being human, there had to be a time when he was alone with God and looked up to heaven and said, "Lord, what's up with this? Where are You in any of this?" Knowing he had done nothing wrong all the way through, set up by his brothers, then that lying woman, Joseph would have had to be thinking, *Wow! I did not see this coming.*

But it was God's next step.

The Lord was with Joseph; Joseph had mercy, favor, and authority. Whatever he did, the Lord prospered. What is the lesson here? Sometimes when we go backward, it is not always because we missed it. It is not always an error. This is a great example of how much our Father loves us. He propelled Joseph backward (at least, it looked that way), but in so doing, He was able to equip and release Joseph into the fullness of his true calling. In this setting, Joseph was equipped to run a nation. All and any pride was stripped from him, and he was humbly trained and shaped to carry the glory of the Lord into this massive calling.

We're going to skip past the dreams in the prison and Joseph's interpretation of those dreams, and how he was still forgotten in prison for another two years after he did all that. You ever hear the saying that time flies? I bet it doesn't in prison or when you are waiting to be launched into ministry, especially when you know there is a God-given call on your life, and you are biting at the bit to get on with it. Look at this:

> Joseph was thirty years old when he stood before Pharaoh
> king of Egypt (Genesis 41:46).

Let's do the math here: Joseph was seventeen when he shared the dreams with his brothers and his father. The Word is clear about that. Joseph was seventeen when he first saw and heard the call of God on his life. It was not a pizza dream. This dream so greatly impacted him that he owned it and felt compelled to share it. We know he was at least two years in prison.

> Then it came to pass, at the end of two full years, that
> Pharaoh had a dream (Genesis 41:1).

Can you imagine having this killer call (metaphorically speaking) on your life? The Lord has spoken to you through two dreams, not one. All you want to do is step into it, and walk it out. The dream was so real, as though you were there. I mean, right there; it was happening right at that very moment. Unfortunately, the dream itself doesn't come with any warnings: you know, something like this, "Yes, My son (or daughter), this is for you. However, it is not going to come to pass for another thirteen years (or in Moses' case, forty years)! But it will happen."

Before I go on, I want to share one of my dreams that is yet to happen. It is so burned into my spirit; it was as if I were there and it was happening all around me. From what I could perceive in the dream, I was moving behind a curtain, a huge curtain. People, lots of people were moving around and doing stuff: These were busy people. I had someone around me fidgeting, adjusting my suit, and I was thinking, *What's up with this?* Then someone handed me a microphone and said, "You're up." I thought, *Up for what?* and the fidgeting person led me toward the curtain. As I was walking toward the front, I stopped. I was standing in front of a dressing mirror. I could see myself, and I thought, *Wow, what a nice suit!* It was so crisp and sharp; it was a two- or three-thousand dollar, tailored suit (I don't know how I knew that, but I did). I was looking and thinking, *Wow, what an awesome looking suit,* when I noticed, *Wow, I am skinny!* I thought, *Now that's a miracle.* And here is the kicker: For the time I was in front of the mirror, I could see everything. I noticed the suit and my weight, but I did not see my face. (Over the years I have contemplated that: *Why not?*) Here it is over twenty years later, and I am still waiting, but now more than ever believing for this day.

Next in the dream as I was led toward the front, the curtain opened, and I was led to the other side of the curtain. I was on a huge platform with a band playing, and they were playing this war dance music. The worship was amazing, and all of a sudden I found myself worshipping and dancing around the platform. At this point, I was thinking, *This is miracles number two and three.* (I don't dance nor can I sing, not because I am too cool, but I just have two left feet and no singing voice.) This day it didn't matter; I was in, I was in with everything I had. Then the music stopped and I looked out, I was stunned, I just stopped. I stared. I was standing at an open-air crusade, and I said, "Lord, what is this?" The next thing I heard was, "It is a sea of people." I said, "What is that?" At that point, I just started preaching. I shared the word that was on my heart and in my spirit. As I was drawing to the end, the Lord said, "Have an altar call," which I did. Tens of thousands (if not more) came forward. Then I was down in the front, and I started praying for people. Suddenly I was bumped and shoved. I looked to my left and there were two big bikers (with colors on their jackets) standing there: one was bigger than the other, but both were large men. The bigger one kept hitting me (more pushing) on the shoulder and saying, "This is rubbish, this is…" (Okay, he didn't use the word "rubbish" but an equivalent.) The guy was adamant that all this was not real. I looked at his friend and the Holy Spirit said to me, "What's wrong with his face?" The guy had been born deformed on the right side of his face. I looked at the guy and said, "What is wrong with your face?" He didn't even get a chance to say anything before I said, "In the name of Jesus, be healed!" Immediately his face was transformed. His eye and all around it was made whole and new. The big dude who was buffeting me fell to his knees, as did the other guy and they both said, "What do we need to do to be saved?" The bikers gave their lives to Jesus right there and then. At that point it was like pandemonium; everyone wanted to be saved. I believe that this will take place in America because the bikers spoke English and I recognized their club as an outlawed club in America.

God is going to move in these clubs. They are also called "one percenters" because they are part of the "one percent" of bikers who are not law-abiding citizens. This means they are regarded as organized crime rings in their countries. Hell's Angels and Sons of Satan are examples, but there are many clubs like this worldwide. God has a plan for them and loves them as much as anyone else. Jesus died and rose again for everyone who will accept Him as Lord and Savior. If there is anything I know about one percenters, it is this: If they believe in something, you ain't changing their minds. I declare that the Lord is going to raise up some of the greatest evangelists ever, and they will come out of the one percenters for such a time as this, the end-time harvest. This was an incredible dream, and brings me to yet another event.

I was having coffee with Jesus one morning and watching the evangelist Reinhard Bonnke on TV. He was doing a crusade in Africa and the cameraman swung the camera out into the crowd. I was shocked, I could not believe what I was seeing. I said to the Lord, "What is that?" The Holy Spirit said, "That is a sea of people" right after that the commentator said, "Will you look at this? It is a sea of people. There are 1.6 million people here today." Tears welled, my spirit leaped. I had had the dream I just shared four years earlier, but it came flooding back to me. The Lord said, "You will see this!" The outpouring that is coming to North America is going to be incredible; the seemingly un-saveable will be preaching; and signs, wonders, and miracles will be commonplace. *People who have been forgiven much will be doing much.* Extreme will be an everyday way of life as the glory of God falls across North America and the world.

I'd like to share one more dream. In this one, I was hovering over a large land mass, and I asked, "Lord, what is this?" Then I saw what looked like a couple of small fires flare up here and there. It started at the lower part of this land mass then they started on the other side. Then I noticed more small fires in the center, then north and south. Again I asked, "Lord, what is this?" I watched in awe as a clear overlay with lines on it came over this land and lowered down upon it. All of a sudden, I thought, *That is California!* (This is where the fires started), then I saw Oregon, Washington, then New York, then way down the eastern coast to Florida, and then Texas. There were fires everywhere. All of a sudden Canada and Mexico had fires everywhere too. Then a huge wind came and all these small fires became one huge, raging, consuming fire and *all of North America was burning.*

Sharing these dreams with others brings me back to Joseph. If the Lord has shown you something totally over the top and you know it is from God, hold onto it and pray about it. Wait on the Lord, as He may not want you to speak it out yet (or at all). Everything has an appointed time:

> To everything there is a season, a time for every purpose under heaven: A time to be born, and a time to die; a time to plant, and a time to pluck what is planted; a time to kill, and a time to heal; a time to break down, and a time to build up; a time to weep, and a time to laugh; a time to mourn, and a time to dance; a time to cast away stones, and a time to gather stones; a time to embrace, and a time to refrain from embracing; a time to gain, and a time to lose; a time to keep, and a time to throw away; a time to tear, and a time to sew; a time to keep silence, and a time to speak; a time to love, and a time to hate; a time of war, and a time of peace. What profit has the worker from that in which he labors? I have seen the God-given task with which the sons of men are to be occupied (Ecclesiastes 3:1-10).

> Then the Lord answered me and said: "Write the vision and make it plain on tablets, that he may run who reads it. For the vision is yet for an appointed time; but at the end it will speak, and it will not lie. Though it tarries, wait for it; because it will surely come, it will not tarry" (Habakkuk 2:2-3).

I, like Joseph, in my zeal had dreams and let them pour out on unbelieving ears, to my own detriment. Thank God my journey wasn't like his! Think about that. All Joseph did was share a dream. Seriously, that was all he did wrong. Look at the outcome! But the Lord had his back. All the naysayers fulfilled his dream in the end through the mighty hand of God. I once heard a preacher speak about "Joseph and the 5 Ps." He said this:

Joseph went from the

1. **P**it (Thrown into a pit to get rid of him.)

To

2. **P**otiphar's (Sold into slavery.)

To

3. **P**rison (Put into prison because he would not sin, but stood righteously.)

To

4. **P**haraoh (Put before the most powerful ruler of his time to help him sort his problems.)

To the

5. **P**alace (Promoted! The Lord exalted him to second-in-command of a nation.)

The Word says:

> Therefore humble yourselves under the mighty hand of God, that He may exalt you in due time (1 Peter 5:6).

All dreams in God are, "Yes and amen." He will fulfill them in the right time; our job is to believe and not lose heart. So I say to you, if you have had dreams from Abba—either a recent one or one that feels like it came an eternity ago, stop, prophesy over your dreams (and the prophetic and personal words over your life spoken from Abba to you). Prophesy and decree them to come alive, to rise up. It is time. We are all to fulfill what is written in our books. It is time to see dreams come alive. It is time to stand up and be all we can be for the Lord. Jesus is waiting for us; we are never waiting on Him. Joseph is one of my heroes. If I could go up to heaven to get some insight from someone other than Jesus, Joseph would be the one, and then Paul, Moses, Joshua, and David too! The dreams God gave you do not lie. *No matter what they look like, choose to believe, and hold on.* We live in a supernatural realm that is about to smash the natural realm and leave people speechless. Don't give up!

> Yet in all these things we are more than conquerors through Him who loved us (Romans 8:37).

Jesus died that we would have life, so trust Him and rise up into the fullness of what you have been called to. Nothing is too hard for Him. We can do all things and walk out every dream to the glory of the Lord. Who can stand before the army of the Lord? We are His army. We are His chosen weapons. It is time to kick butt. Every God-given dream has an appointed time, and though it tarry, *it will surely come*. It will not tarry forever. I am still waiting on some dreams from twenty years ago or longer. I have been called everything under the sun by all sorts of people (mainly brothers and sisters, unfortunately). I am convinced more now than ever that it is time to see these dreams come to pass, and for that I praise the Lord. I believe and I receive everything I have prayed for according to Mark 11: 23-24:

> For assuredly, I say to you, whoever says to this mountain, "Be removed and be cast into the sea," and does not doubt in his heart, but believes that those things he says will be done, he will have whatever he says. Therefore I say to you, whatever things you ask when you pray, believe that you receive them, and you will have them.

Join me in prayer:

> *Father, we pray over every dream and prophetic word ever spoken over us, and we say, "Come alive now, in Jesus' name!" Jesus, I plead Your blood over each and every dream and prophetic word that is from You. Seal them in Your blood now. I ask, Jesus, that You would strengthen us who have been waiting for a long time, that we will believe and hold on for the appointed day to see Your glory upon our lives, according to your Word which*

says, 'No weapon formed against you shall prosper, and every tongue which rises against you in judgment You shall condemn. This is the heritage of the servants of the Lord, and their righteousness is from Me, says the Lord' (Isaiah 54:17). So no weapon formed against us shall prosper, and every tongue which rises against us, we condemn. Father, we condemn every negative or cursing word spoken against us in Jesus' name, so we may rise up into the fullness of our call. Thank You, Lord. Amen.

What if, like Joseph, we held onto our dreams? What if we pushed through and did everything unto the Lord, no matter what it looked like? Joseph lived an extreme life; no matter what it looked like, he persevered. Could you imagine what would have happened if he would have let that lying woman and her accusations crush him? What if he would have said, "Lord, my brothers did me wrong. I can't do this, I'm done. I quit; it's over"? His story would not even be in the Bible! But the Lord knew Joseph would rise up and follow Him first! What if we could all get past the trials, the testings, the judgments, the criticisms, the lies, and in some cases, the well it's-just-too-hard scenarios? If the Lord has shown you something and it is 100% from Him, it will happen. However, there will be a shaping process beforehand. This is so you can carry the glory of the Lord when you are ready to fulfill your destiny to glorify His name. Come on, I encourage everyone reading this to run with what the Lord has given you. There is An Extreme Walk With Jesus! Don't Settle For Second Best!

Chapter Four: "Tell Them I Am Coming!"

L ast night I had a dream and woke to the words, "Tell them I am coming! Tell them I am coming! Tell them I am coming!" It was so loud, so clear and precise. The funny part was that I couldn't remember the dream, but the mandate was like crystal. There was no gray area here. Jesus is the soon and coming King, the Rider on the white horse, faithful and true. After lying there for a long time, as I couldn't go back to sleep, I meditated on this word. This overwhelming urgency kept coming to me. It was not a, "I'll be there in a hundred or so years. It was a get ready. *Tell them I am coming!"*

> But concerning the times and the seasons, brethren, you have no need that I should write to you. For you yourselves know perfectly that the day of the Lord so comes as a thief in the night. For when they say, "Peace and safety!" then sudden destruction comes upon them, as labor pains upon a pregnant woman. And they shall not escape. But you, brethren, are not in darkness, so that this Day should overtake you as a thief (1 Thessalonians 5:1-4).

As I laid in bed, unable to sleep, I was led by the Spirit to write this chapter. All these scriptures kept going through my mind:

> But of that day and hour no one knows, not even the angels of heaven, but My Father only. But as the days of Noah were, so also will the coming of the Son of Man be. For as in the days before the flood, they were

eating and drinking, marrying and giving in marriage, until the day that Noah entered the ark, and did not know until the flood came and took them all away, so also will the coming of the Son of Man be. Then two men will be in the field: one will be taken and the other left. Two women will be grinding at the mill: one will be taken and the other left. Watch therefore, for you do not know what hour your Lord is coming. But know this, that if the master of the house had known what hour the thief would come, he would have watched and not allowed his house to be broken into. Therefore you also be ready, for the Son of Man is coming at an hour you do not expect (Matthew 24:36-44).

I tell you, on that night two people will be in one bed; one will be taken and the other left. Two women will be grinding grain together; one will be taken and the other left (Luke 17:34-36 NIV).

Jesus is speaking in both of these verses. He is warning of how His return will be swift and unexpected; and more importantly, He is saying how many are going to be taken by surprise and not be ready. If this was the only thing Jesus said on the subject, you might think, *Okay, I got it*. But this is not the case. Jesus goes on to speak about the faithful servant and the evil servant, the parable of the wise and foolish virgins, then the parable of the talents. Jesus was truly making a point here about being ready.

The body of Christ is not ready—not even close. There are so many seeker-friendly and hyper-grace churches because we do not want to offend people. We have become so politically correct that we now tolerate sin. We do not speak about the blood enough (or at all), and it is through the blood we are set free! Nor do we speak about sin and what it is; nor the fruit of the Spirit or speaking in tongues and the power of that. Our auditoriums (or sanctuaries) have become nightclubs: smoke-filled rooms with music so loud that some people have to wear earplugs or stand outside until praise and worship is over. It is all justified by "we are trying to reach the youth."

What if we just got back to worshipping Jesus, got sin out of our lives, preached Jesus and the kingdom of God, and that the kingdom of God is at hand? What if we became the uncompromising body of Christ we are supposed to be, preparing the church for the return of Jesus? If we are worshipping Him in Spirit and truth and washed in the blood, then we will see smoke, but it won't be from a machine. It will be the glory, the "kabod" glory of God. The Hebrew word *kabod* originally meant the "weight" or "heaviness" of God.[5]

We don't need to imitate the world with a nightclub style or any other worldly trappings to reach the youth or any other people group. We need the *kabod* glory, the presence of Almighty God to show up. The lost are looking for the supernatural, something that will impact and transform their lives. There has never been such a search for the supernatural as there is today. You see it everywhere. Every year there are multiple movies and TV shows on the supernatural; it's in the media, magazines, and books. People are searching for answers. For them to go to a nightclub on a Saturday night, and then go to a church on Sunday and see some of the same people they just saw in the nightclub, doing exactly what they were doing, isn't life-changing or transforming. It does not offer them any hope for change. We need to get completely free from man-pleasing and being seeker-friendly, and get back to preaching the Word like Jesus did. I know some think times are different, and it is not the same anymore, but Jesus is the same and always will be. "Jesus is the same yesterday, today, and forever." He preached and lived an uncompromising life, and we are to do the same. *What if we got back to our first love?* Got our eyes off the world, focused them back on Jesus, and let the Holy Spirit be in charge again? What do I mean? Here's an example: My friends were telling me about this new church they were attending (for a short period), and how it works with all its special formats and programs. As this is a fairly big church with multiple

---

5. James Strong, "3519b. Kabod," Biblehub.com, accessed March 01, 2019, https://biblehub.com/hebrew/3519b.htm.

meetings on a Sunday, it was explained to my friends by a couple of the church's pastors that they like to move in the Spirit, but only the Spirit wearing a seat belt. I didn't mean to, but I started laughing. Seriously think about that: "Holy Spirit, You are welcome here, but we have to be out by 10:30, so do what You gotta do, but not too long; oh, and nothing messy. Please wear a seat belt, so things don't get out of control."

Sometimes it just has to get messy before it gets clean. We need to get back to preaching the *uncompromised* Word and let the Holy Spirit have His way. When the glory of God shows up in a church, it is wonderful for young and old. People get saved; people get healed and delivered; people get set free and then the church fills. Where the tangible glory of the Lord is, there is fruit—and the fruit speaks for itself. God gets the glory, the name of Jesus is exalted, and the Holy Spirit is free to move. A few weeks after an evangelist had visited, Pastor Graham said that the sign of a good evangelist is that it takes weeks, even months, to clean up what the man of God stirred up.

I once ministered at a church in Queensland, Australia. The worship started, the offering was taken, I preached, and started ministering, and the whole service went on for four-and-a-half to five hours. It was awesome. About an hour into ministering, the pastor said, "This is getting a little long." I replied, "If this is man, people will get bored and leave and it will be finished, but if this is God, everyone will stay until it is over." Then I stopped and told everyone that if anyone needed to go, they were released. Everyone stayed. In fact, people would get out of a prayer line, go downstairs, have a cappuccino at the church café, come back upstairs, step back in line, and wait. When the Lord moves, He moves. The last person I prayed over was at the four-and-a-half to five-hour mark. I ministered to 97% of the church, one by one. Two or three months later I was still getting reports back from the pastor as to the lives that had been transformed. Praise the Lord! I was asked back a few times after that. It was awesome to allow the Holy Spirit to move as He saw fit. Only the Holy Spirit can transform us through Jesus Christ to the glory of the Father. Yes, the Word does say to let all things be done in order, but let's look at that for a minute;

> Therefore, brethren, desire earnestly to prophesy, and do
> not forbid to speak with tongues. Let all things be done
> decently and in order (1 Corinthians 14:39-40).

This is speaking about tongues, interpretation of tongues, and prophecy. It is not speaking about bridling the Holy Spirit or giving Him a seat belt. That would just be "ludicrous." This is not a word I often use. In fact, I didn't know how to spell it, and I thought it meant crazy. However I looked it up and, wow! Look at the meaning:

> **Ludicrous:** So foolish, unreasonable, or out of place as
> to be amusing. (Synonyms: absurd, ridiculous, laughable,
> preposterous.)[6]

To harness the Holy Spirit is truly ludicrous! The Father speaks from heaven, saying, "Let there be light," and boom! The Holy Spirit moves, and there is light. The Father says, "Let Us make man in Our image," and it is done. We say, Lord, release the harvest, send us the lost, and the Holy Spirit starts to move. Believe me, it will get messy—and I mean messy. Some of the leaders and heavy tithers will come to the pastor and try to shut down a move of God, threatening to leave (with their money), saying, "We don't like this; it is messy and uncomfortable. This cannot be God." I have seen this happen in more than one church. It is ridiculous, but this problem is real.

Some choose to deny the move of the Spirit. I understand that we need to govern our flesh, because when we don't, it can be distracting—even annoying, for a lack of better words. But the issue here revolves around giving the Holy Spirit control. We truly need to be careful when the Holy Spirit starts to move and we say that it isn't God. In Toronto, then Brownsville, and other places, many people came against those moves for months only to jump in later, like they were there from the beginning. Others are still condemning moves that are actually bearing

---

6. "Ludicrous | Definition of Ludicrous in English by Oxford Dictionaries," Oxford Dictionaries | English, accessed March 08, 2019, https://en.oxforddictionaries.com/definition/ludicrous.

fruit and setting people free today! Our theology does not always fit with what happens in the Spirit. The new move of God that is coming will be incredible—unlike anything we've ever seen before. A new thing that will leave some denying it is God. Be careful, very careful, and be sensitive to the Holy Spirit. When the glory of the Lord is unleashed for the end-time harvest, it is going to be absolutely fantastic.

The Word says, "eyes have not seen" or ears have not heard the things God is about to do. This end-time harvest is going to look like nothing we have ever seen before.

> But as it is written: "Eye has not seen, nor ear heard, nor
> have entered into the heart of man the things which God
> has prepared for those who love Him" (1 Corinthians 2:9).

Call it what you will (I call it outstanding), but it is time to rock the world. I am very excited for what is coming. I don't care what it looks like as long as it is from God and people's lives are being saved and transformed for His glory. *Lock and load, people! It is coming, and so is Jesus.* I am ecstatic just thinking about the tsunami of glory about to be released upon the earth. It's ludicrous *not* to want to walk in this glory or be part of it. Think about it: The last chapter of the book is unfolding. This is the most exciting time in history to be alive; He is coming! Jesus is seriously coming, so don't be caught sleeping. Don't miss what has been written in your book. We are living in crazy demanding times, yet there is a bigger picture. Ask the Lord to show you. He is waiting for us to stand up and say, "Pick me, send me! If you are thinking, *John, I am not so sure about that. If God wants me, He can come and get me because I'm right here*, consider these verses: (At different times in my walk, I thought that too, by the way.)

> For the eyes of the Lord run to and fro throughout
> the whole earth, to show Himself strong on behalf
> of those whose heart is loyal to Him (2 Chronicles 16:9a).

> Also I heard the voice of the Lord, saying: "Whom shall
> I send, and who will go for Us?" Then I said, "Here am I!
> Send me" (Isaiah 6:8).

This should be the call of all our hearts: "Here am I! Send me."
I believe if we truly had the revelation of where we were in history,
where we stand in the time line of prophecy, written thousands of years
ago, we would not be so concerned with "keeping up with the Joneses."
Everyone knows the Jones family with their humongous house, two of
the biggest, shiniest cars on the planet, the yacht, and the maxed-out
credit cards. It's all gonna burn. Don't get me wrong, I believe in the
blessing of the Lord and that we are the seed of Abraham through Jesus
Christ of Nazareth, heirs of the promise who share in the inheritance of
Abraham. We are blessed beyond the wildest imagination, but here is a
problem with all that. *It's awesome only if it is paid for.*

I have some friends who have had prophetic words about being debt-
free spoken over them. God wanted them to owe nothing to anyone so
they could be prepared for what is coming.

> Owe no one anything except to love one another, for he
> who loves another has fulfilled the law (Romans 13:8).

Just the other day I was talking to them about it again, and I said,
"Here is the issue. You both love the Lord with all your hearts; that
isn't even in question. You both believe you are called to something
greater than what you are currently doing and what you have done so
far. Let me give you a hypothetical example, as this is rampant in the
body of Christ. The Lord says to a married couple, "I want you to go to
Africa for six months. You will see amazing things, and I will be with
you. Will you do it?" This couple looked at each other and said, "We
could not do the will of the Father. We just couldn't go! We could not
do it and continue paying the mortgage payment, the SUV payment, the
truck payment, and the credit cards." (Suddenly they felt in bondage.)
This husband feels enslaved to a job which pays well, but he does not
love, and his wife had to go to work to help pay for all their debt. They
wanted to follow the calling on their lives to serve the Lord, but they are

trapped, enslaved to the Babylonian system. The Devil has sucked them into a lifestyle which they mistakenly believed was the blessing of the Lord to have all this stuff. But *you don't have stuff until it is paid for*. Then it is yours, and no one can take it. God wants you to have stuff, believe me. He just does not want it to come through pain and bondage to get it.

> But seek first the kingdom of God and His righteousness, and all these things shall be added to you (Matthew 6:33).

Now that this couple has realized the problem, they want to serve the Lord with everything they have. They can't quit their jobs though; they have to pay their debt. They can't get six months off work to go either, that's too long. The financial pressure they are under is starting show. It is bringing pressure into the marriage and the family. All this time they believed that they were walking out a prosperous Christian life, but the reality was that they were bound by debt. They have very little equity in their home. They have to pay for their vehicles and credit cards. Even if they wanted to serve God, they can't in their present circumstance.

> The blessing of the Lord makes one rich, and He adds no sorrow with it (Proverbs 10:22).

> No one can serve two masters; for either he will hate the one and love the other, or else he will be loyal to the one and despise the other. You cannot serve God and mammon (Matthew 6:24).

Why am I saying this? Well, it is simple: *Jesus is coming, and He is coming soon.* The Devil has too many God-fearing, God-loving men and woman bound up so they cannot fulfill the fullness of their calls because the Devil has them chasing the things of the world. Too many are so far in debt that they have deceived themselves, believing themselves blessed by God but still in debt. Do I believe in the blessing of the Lord? Absolutely, and when He blesses you "He adds no sorrow with it."

I explained to this couple that the reason the Lord was telling them to get out of debt was because He wanted to use them. If they owed no money and the only debt they had was to love, God could take them anywhere and use them in ways that would blow their minds. I believe God will help them and they will still realize their call to Africa.

When God is in it, we can go anywhere for the Lord as outstanding men and women of faith. Do I believe in debt? Personally for me, no, but that is for me. The Lord told me to get out of debt and stay out of debt twenty years ago. He told me to owe no man anything except for to love. A couple times along the way, I did go into debt, but it never worked out well for me. Even when I was making good money and things were going well, my means dried up as soon as I borrowed money, and then I struggled to pay the debt back. When I took this struggle to the Lord, I asked Him why I was having so much trouble. He told me it was because He had told me not to go into debt in the first place.

I have no mortgage, no car payments, no credit-card debt, and only a few small soon-to-be-paid personal debts—but I have freedom. I can go anywhere He sends me. I am believing for a house, cars, and the things we need, but I am believing that God will pay for them as in:

> Even so the Lord has commanded that those who preach the gospel should live from the gospel (1 Corinthians 9:14).

> For the Scripture says, "You shall not muzzle an ox while it treads out the grain," and, "The laborer is worthy of his wages" (1 Timothy 5:18).

And my favorite:

> Then Peter began to say to Him, "See, we have left all and followed You." So Jesus answered and said, "Assuredly, I say to you, there is no one who has left house or brothers or sisters or father or mother or wife or children or lands, for My sake and the gospel's, who shall not receive a hundredfold now in this time—houses and

brothers and sisters and mothers and children and lands, with persecutions—and in the age to come, eternal life. But many who are first will be last, and the last first" (Mark 10:28-31).

The fruit of the [consistently] righteous is a tree of life, and he who is wise captures and wins souls [for God—he gathers them for eternity]...the righteous will be rewarded on the earth [with godly blessings] (Proverbs 11:30-31a AMP).

If Jesus said it, I believe it. I have had dreams of my house (the one He will give me). I have seen it. One day when my pastor was praying for me, he saw it. Over the years I have had five or six different people come up to me and say, "I had a dream last night. I don't know where it is, but I came to your house to visit you, and..." Then each one has described it the same way, seeing the same things. One thing I know for sure is that if the Lord wants me to have a house, He will pay for it. It will be debt-free and it will only be a base, a place to rest and prepare between traveling and preaching. I am okay with that.

Am I saying all debt is wrong? No, I believe this is for me because that is what the Holy Spirit told me to do. Debt is between you and God. All I know is that many sincere Christians who want to serve the Lord with everything they have, can't do it because they are financially strapped. It only pleases their fleshly desires and is not meeting their spiritual ones. I heard a preacher once say, "The only thing you can take to heaven with you is souls." (I think it was Reinhard Bonnke.) It doesn't get any more real than that.

Time is short. Jesus is coming back and way sooner than any of us think. He is coming and He is coming soon. What are you going to do with the time you have left here on earth?

We are in the world but we are not part of the world; we are just passing through, sojourners and aliens here. This is not our home. We are not supposed to get comfortable. We have a mission, a destiny to fulfill. We need to be telling this dying world of the hope they can have in the soon and coming King. We need to be reaping a harvest because it is ripe and waiting.

"Tell them I am coming?" Well, I have done that in this chapter: Jesus is coming. He is coming soon. We need to be telling everyone we come across that Jesus is coming, so get ready!

If you have found yourself in this exact situation (in debt and not able to reach the things you feel you are to accomplish), it is not the end of the world.

Pray this with me, I have prayed this myself:

> *Lord, I come to You, and if I have gotten myself (and my family) into a world of debt that is not of You. I repent now. I ask forgiveness for going into debt. Father, in Jesus' name, my heart is to serve You with everything I have. I ask for Your wisdom and strategies to get me (and my family) out of this debt. Lord, I thank You for Your grace and mercy in this situation. I thank You, Lord, that You are the God of the impossible and that nothing is impossible for You. I trust that You have my back and that I will see Your glory in all this. I love You, Lord. We know that all things work together for good to those who love You, to those who are called according to Your purpose. Lord, I believe I am called according to Your purpose, and I ask You to move swiftly in this so I can serve You with everything I have. Deliver me (and my family) from this weight of debt, in Jesus' name. Amen.*

What if we really could believe Jesus is coming, I mean really coming and soon? Does that idea change the way we think, the way we do things? Would it bring us to the place of saying, "Lord, I repent for wasting time. Please set me on fire for You, Lord. I ask for great boldness to tell people You are coming, and coming soon. Lord, let me be extreme in this. Abba, do not let me miss one person that You have written in my book. May I share You with everyone that You put before me. Let Your will become mine. Lord, I have heard that You are coming and You are coming soon"?

I wasn't always where I am today. It has been a long journey; but if I can do it, anyone can. It is God in me who has brought me where I am today, but I did have to do my bit (surrender everything). May we join one another in this. May we serve Him together with all our hearts, no matter how long our journeys are.

Chapter Five: Witty Ideas

(The Sovereign Hand of God)

> A good man leaves an inheritance to his children's children, and the wealth of the sinner is stored up for [the hands of] the righteous (Proverbs 13:22 AMP).

I am excited to share what the Lord has spoken to me on this subject. Let's look at the Big Picture: One billion plus souls are about to be saved. It is going to take hundreds of billions of dollars, if not trillions, to reap this harvest. The exciting part of all this is that Abba wants to use us, not only to reap souls, but to reap a harvest of unprecedented finances—the like of which has never been seen before! We are to plunder hell to populate heaven; that is going to take resources. Can God do this? Think about the scripture above. We know everything has to line up with the Word. Where has God done this before? Is this only found in one place?

> Now the children of Israel had done according to the word of Moses, and they had asked from the Egyptians articles of silver, articles of gold, and clothing. And the Lord had given the people favor in the sight of the Egyptians, so that they granted them what they requested. Thus they plundered the Egyptians (Exodus 12:35-36).

Hmmm, sounds like the wealth of the wicked were stored up for the righteous there too.

> And when he had brought him down, there they were, spread out over all the land, eating and drinking and dancing, because of all the great spoil which they had taken from the land of the Philistines and from the land of Judah. Then David attacked them from twilight until the evening of the next day. Not a man of them escaped, except four hundred young men who rode on camels and fled. So David recovered all that the Amalekites had carried away, and David rescued his two wives. And nothing of theirs was lacking, either small or great, sons or daughters, spoil or anything which they had taken from them; David recovered all. Then David took all the flocks and herds they had driven before those other livestock, and said, "This is David's spoil" (1 Samuel 30:16-20).

Amazing! Here's David out doing his thing, and his city gets raided: Everything is taken (women, children, gold, silver, and livestock, the lot); but even in this, the Lord protects David's people and things. It's a little rough on David though. He is a hero one minute and his men want to kill him the next.

> Now it happened, when David and his men came to Ziklag, on the third day, that the Amalekites had invaded the South and Ziklag, attacked Ziklag and burned it with fire, and had taken captive the women and those who were there, from small to great; they did not kill anyone, but carried them away and went their way. So David and his men came to the city, and there it was, burned with fire; and their wives, their sons, and their daughters had been taken captive. Then David and the people who were with him lifted up their voices and wept, until they had no more power to weep. And David's two wives, Ahinoam the Jezreelitess, and Abigail the widow of Nabal the Carmelite, had been taken captive. Now David was greatly distressed, for the people spoke of stoning him, because the soul

of all the people was grieved, every man for his sons and his daughters. But David strengthened himself in the Lord his God (1 Samuel 30:1-6).

What did David do? He strengthened himself in the Lord his God.

When you read this you have to look at it for what it is: David could have just said, "Lord, I know You have called me, but this is just a little too hard. One minute these guys You gave me love me, and the next minute they want to whack me. I give up, I can't do this, Lord." But nope, that's not what David did. Don't get me wrong, the Word says that "David was greatly distressed (hmm, depressed), for the people spoke of stoning him." This was not a good day at the office. But instead of giving up, David goes before the Lord; he needs a word from the Lord—a plan or a strategy. David inquires of the Lord; he seeks His face and presses into the Lord. *He does not give up!*

Then David said to Abiathar the priest, Ahimelech's son, "Please bring the ephod here to me." And Abiathar brought the ephod to David. So David inquired of the Lord, saying, "Shall I pursue this troop? Shall I overtake them?" And He answered him, "Pursue, for you shall surely overtake them and without fail recover all." (1 Samuel 30:7-8).

David did exactly what the Lord said. He not only recovered what was taken from him and his people, but if you read carefully, it says this: *"Then David took all the flocks and herds they had driven before those other* livestock.*"* David not only got his stuff back, but all the spoils from the raiders, meaning the things they had taken from other villages and cities. Hallelujah!

There may be some reading this right now who have had stuff taken by the enemy. Some things were lost of your own doing and some were taken by the enemy in his attempts to get you to give up or quit. He's been trying to crush your destiny, and you may have lost everything. It could be houses, cars, finances, a job, a wife, a husband, children, family, or whatever. You need to stand up (and I mean literally stand up) right now, and decree, declare and demand that the scumbag (the Devil) has to back up and let go now, in Jesus' name.

> Therefore submit to God. Resist the devil and he will flee from you (James 4:7).

You need to let him know you are never giving up. Pray this:

> *Father, I pray this over my life and everything around me:* "Our Father in heaven, hallowed be Your name. *(Stomp your feet and **declare** this like you are fighting for your life **because you are!**)* Your kingdom come. Your will be done on earth as it is *in heaven. Oh, God, that Your will, will be done in my life (and my family's) on earth as in heaven. May what is written in my book be manifest in the natural here, according to Your will in heaven.* Give us our daily bread day by day. And forgive us our sins, for we also forgive everyone who is indebted to us. And do not lead us into temptation, but deliver us from the evil one."

If you are reading this and saying to yourself, *It is too late, it is over. This all sounds good, but I have lost everything and I am at rock bottom,* consider this: There just ain't nowhere else to go. Look at David! His guys wanted to stone him and they weren't at all happy. They wanted him stoned—to death. That's rock bottom. Yet David sought the Lord, and the Lord gave David a plan, a strategy, a way out. David did what the Lord instructed and he got everything back and more, and all his men loved him again. *What God did for David, He will do for you too!*

There is hope! It may not look like it, but this is where we have to believe.

> Be strong and of good courage, do not fear nor be afraid of them; for the Lord your God, He is the One who

goes with you. He will not leave you nor forsake you (Deuteronomy 31:6).

For He has said, "I will never [under any circumstances] desert you [nor give you up nor leave you without support, nor will I in any degree leave you helpless], nor will I forsake or let you down or relax My hold on You [assuredly not]!" So we take comfort and are encouraged and confidently say, "The Lord is my Helper [in time of need], I will not be afraid. What will man do to me?" (Hebrews 13:5-6 AMP).

Are you feeling it? Brother, Sister, there is a breakthrough on the way! It is coming—just like Jesus. The Lord is not finished with you, not even close. In fact, He hasn't even started: Everything to this point has been a testing and proving time, a time of shaping, a preparing time. I don't care how long you have been saved or where you are as a Christian or if you are at the top or the bottom: There is always more in God, much more—an infinity. The day we think we have it all together is the day we are truly in trouble. Brother, Sister, look at Moses! He thought he was the deliverer of his people. He killed a guy, then spent forty years in the desert. I imagine there were days when he thought, *Man, this is just way too hard.* Then he rescued his people, only to walk in the wilderness with a few million stiff-necked sheep for forty more years! Talk about a hard walk.

I have waited a long time to walk in the fullness of my call, and I have been at rock bottom a few times. I have thought, *It's too hard! I can't do this anymore.* I have had the Devil whispering in my ear, "You're a loser. None of this will ever happen. Did God really say that? Oh, that's a good one! Look at you! You will never go to the nations. You're getting too old." To all these words I had to apply James 4:7 a million times (and this is only a slight exaggeration). So resist the Devil with the Word of God, and he *has to flee!* It is true!

The Word of God is powerful like nothing else. One day when I was feeling sorry for myself, Deuteronomy 8 turned my head upside down.

I know I am not the only one who has ever felt like that either. God led me to read it, and I got as far as verse 2 and couldn't get past it. I had read this chapter many times, but suddenly saw it in a new light. I now meditate on it frequently. On the day it hit me, I was feeling abandoned and forsaken, kicked to the curb. Joseph had to have had days like that too. The Word doesn't tell us, but what could it have been like for Joseph to have had such amazing dreams, only to end up in prison? Joseph must have wondered, *How could this happen?* Those are the times that try us most. This is what I read:

> And you shall remember that the Lord your God led you all the way these forty years in the wilderness, to humble you and test you, to know what was in your heart, whether you would keep His commandments or not (Deuteronomy 8:2).

God humbles and tests us: It says so! Like I said, I had read that chapter many times; but until that day, I just always paid more attention to the good parts about blessing and wealth and restoration instead. I thank God that not everyone has to lose everything to be tried and tested. Not everyone must go through desert years to know what's in their heart; but everyone does go through *some* wilderness experiences. There were days I would scream at the Lord. (What?) Yep, you read that right: I screamed at the Lord: "Lord, I can't do this anymore! Take me home; this is too hard." When you're feeling down, verses about being humbled and tested do not feel encouraging; and I was feeling down, lower than the dirt. Still in the middle of it all, I heard the Holy Spirit say, "I will not allow you to be tempted beyond what you can handle." Of course, I did not agree, and yelled back, saying that I could not handle it, yet everything the Lord brought into my life, as hard as some of it was, made me stronger when I came out on the other side. Looking back, I see that I actually needed those hard times. Most of those experiences were lonely too. Unfortunately, no one can walk your wilderness journey with you. Many times the Holy Spirit told me these words: *"If I bring you to it, I will bring you through it!"* It's nice to hear that now, but it wasn't at the time.

No temptation [regardless of its source] has overtaken or enticed you that is not common to human experience [nor is any temptation unusual or beyond human resistance]; but God is faithful [to His word—He is compassionate and trustworthy], and He will not let you be tempted beyond your ability [to resist], but along with the temptation He [has in the past and is now and] will [always] provide the way out as well, so that you will be able to endure it [without yielding, and will overcome temptation with joy] (1 Corinthians 10:13 AMP).

The temptation I am referring to here is quitting, giving up, or packing it in, but this verse applies to *all* temptation: addiction, sin, or anything else. There were many times when I wanted to fold under pressure. I wanted to tell the Lord to find some other dude. This was all just way too hard. Yes, I was having quite the pity party. I often looked at others and compared my circumstances with theirs. I couldn't see anyone else going through anything like this. One day Pastor Graham said to me, "John, I have never seen anyone go through as much stuff as you have. You are hardly out of one thing and bang, you're right into something else. The Lord just keeps dealing with stuff in your life, and here you are: still standing. All by yourself, but still standing!" He got excited and said, "I just saw the cover of your first book and the title is *Still Standing!*

There are people reading this right now who are feeling rejected, abandoned, hopeless, lost, destitute, even suicidal. You have lost your vision or it now seems unattainable. Perhaps you even wonder if it ever was God's plan at all. Everyone has left you or abandoned you, called you a dreamer and worse. Some may have accused you of arrogance and pride, or judged you as ignorant because you shared your dreams and they did not understand them. Believe it or not, you are in the best place you could ever be: in the hand of the Lord. The Lord is about to promote you; He is about to lift you up. He is about to shine through you like never before. All your God-given dreams, plans, ideas, and inventions will come forth. Oh, my brother and sister, the Lord would say:

"This is not the time to give up! It is time to press into Me like never before. Do not look to the right or the left; look up, for that is where I am found. Have I not said, 'I will never leave nor forsake you all the days of your life'? Well, I mean it! My plans for you are to do you good, not harm. My plans are to prosper you, to give you a hope and future. This is the hour when I will download My plans and strategies from heaven. Look to Me, the Author and Finisher of your faith. I am going to use you for My glory in these last days; it is not over. Do not look at your present circumstances: Look to Me! I am the Game Changer! I have every day of your life written for you; I know the plans I have for you. Arise, shine for My glory has come upon you. I will use you as I have shown you, so seek Me while I may be found, says the Lord."

> Arise, shine; for your light has come! And the glory of the Lord is risen upon you. For behold, the darkness shall cover the earth, and deep darkness the people; but the Lord will arise over you, and His glory will be seen upon you. The Gentiles shall come to your light, and kings to the brightness of your rising. Lift up your eyes all around, and see: They all gather together, they come to you; your sons shall come from afar, and your daughters shall be nursed at your side. Then you shall see and become radiant, and your heart shall swell with joy; because the abundance of the sea shall be turned to you, the wealth of the Gentiles shall come to you... Therefore your gates shall be open continually; they shall not be shut day or night, that men may bring to you the wealth of the Gentiles, and their kings in procession (Isaiah 60:1-5, 11).

Look, whether you are down and out and looking at life with your natural eyes, or soaring with the eagles, I have great news. The Lord is about to turn this world upside down, and we are about to see the wealth of the Gentiles come into the kingdom. This will begin with those with a Matthew 6:33 mentality, those seeking first His kingdom and His righteousness. I foresee a people who enter into a kingdom reversal.

They will give ninety percent into the kingdom and will not be able to spend the whole ten percent that is left for them and their families because it will be *too much*. If you are not excited about this, check for a pulse. There are many different ways this is going to unfold. Here's a few the Lord has shown me:

Inventions: The Lord is going to download ideas for inventions into people. These will be in the automotive, sciences, agriculture, oil exploration, energy, health, and many other areas. God's glory will be seen in His people.

Plans: He is going to grant blueprints for struggling companies: plans on how to turn dying companies around (kind of like a Daniel and Joseph thing). In return for saving a company, people will be rewarded with either shares in the company, the company itself, or a paycheck. There is a Christian guy in Australia who does this now. He was once paid one million dollars to write a mission statement for a company. God gave it to Him in fifteen minutes, but it turned the company around. He has been paid by many businesses to write their mission statements: not bad for a guy who was illiterate when he was seventeen. All wisdom belongs to God, so ask Him for it!

> If any of you lacks wisdom, you should ask God, who gives generously to all without finding fault, and it will be given to you (James 1:5 NIV).

Real Estate: The Lord is going to open doors for His people to buy land and develop it, or simply have people give land to Christian business people. For others, unfinished projects and complexes and/ or failed investments will become available and they will experience record sales. Homes will be picked up for a song and sold for a profit.

> Jabez prayed to the God of Israel: "Bless me, O bless me! Give me land, large tracts of land. And provide your personal protection—don't let evil hurt me." God gave him what he asked (1 Chronicles 4:10 MSG).

Strategies: He will show others how to invest their finance to reap a thirty-, sixty- and hundredfold return. It is time we believe that the three-to-nine percent return isn't God, and luck has nothing to do with any of it. The Lord is going to show people companies that are about to go public. They will invest (buy shares) in them prior to their launch and see a hundredfold increase and more. The Lord will show others start-up companies that they should invest in, and then they will watch those companies explode with profit. The Holy Spirit will lead people to invest in the stock market. He will tell them when to buy, what to buy, and when to sell. Being close with the Holy Spirit will be hugely important in this. If you miss it, you'll lose it.

Witty Ideas: Others will take inventions and polish them: either making them more efficient or putting different things together in ways not imagined before, possibly even with new purposes in mind. I have an example of this:

One night I woke and sat straight up in bed and said, "That was the strangest dream!" Then I heard (I'm not sure if it was audible, but it was loud and clear), "This is not a dream. It is a witty idea straight from the strategy room of heaven! Write it down exactly how you saw it!" So I did. I wrote exactly what I saw. For months, I would read it over and over, thinking, *Wow, this is so cool.* About six months later, I asked the Holy Spirit, "This is all good and stuff, but what am I supposed to *do* with this?" The Holy Spirit said, "I want you to make a commercial exactly as you saw in the dream." I thought, *Cool, Lord, but there are a couple of issues with this plan. First of all, I don't know anything about making a commercial, and secondly, I have no money. Interesting.*

Has the Lord asked you to do something that seems utterly impossible? If He hasn't, He will! It is so exciting too! For a week or so, I spent time before the Lord, asking Him how I should pull off this enormously daunting task. The Lord had stretched my faith to believe for the impossible many times before, but this was huge. As I sought the Lord for an answer, it seemed like I was getting nothing and going nowhere. I went to bed, knowing I had to get up early to go to a business breakfast by 6:30 a.m. I was so preoccupied with what seemed impossible, that I did not even want to go the next morning. I just wanted to figure this thing out instead. When I got there, I was greeted by the guy in charge, and went to look for a place to sit. I thought maybe I should sit near the back, and saw a guy I knew and decided to sit beside him. Peter was doing some work before the meeting, so we said hi and he continued working. Another dude came in who also knew Peter and he came and sat one chair away from me, leaving a space. This guy introduced himself as Ben. Ben was kind-of chatty, and asked me all sorts of questions. I was preoccupied and didn't feel up to the conversation, but Ben persisted so I finally asked him, "So Ben, what do you do?" After this, no one could ever convince me that the Lord did not have our every day planned—even when it doesn't seem like it at all.

Ben looked at me and said, "I own a production company." Not really thinking any further, I casually continued, "What do you produce?" He answered, "I do different things. I do streaming, documentaries, and company video, as well as commercials." I thought, *No way!* So I said, "This may sound weird (Actually a lot of my conversations start that way) but I had a dream…" I shared the dream and then said, "I waited on the Lord, and He has instructed me to do a commercial, exactly the way I saw it. What would something like that cost?" Ben explained that it would cost somewhere between $10,000 to $20,000, give or take a little. I thought, *Wow, Lord!* Things got quiet for ten to fifteen minutes, and then Ben said, "John, the Lord told me to do this for you, and I am only to charge you for my cost (his time)." I was thinking *Cool!* Then Peter lifted his head from his work. He had heard everything. He looked at Ben and said, "Send me the invoice." The Lord told Peter to pay for it! This was one hundred percent God! I almost didn't go to that breakfast because I was so concerned about getting this thing done, yet had no way of doing it. I almost missed it! Sometimes you just have to be at the right place at the right time doing the right thing and meeting the right people. You just have to be doing what you are supposed to be doing to see God's hands move.

In conclusion, the witty idea was completed; it was a state-of-the-art security system. Next I asked the Lord what I was to do with it. He told me to send it to a guy named Joe in a well-known ministry in America and wait. I did the first part; and when Joe looked at it, he was blown away. When he watched it, he called in someone else who was walking by and they both watched it together. The other person told Joe this: "That is straight out of the throne room! That is truly a witty idea!" To make a long story short, I didn't wait as I ought to have. I listened to man and not God and lost the whole thing: An Australian company ended up with it. There's more to this story, but I will leave that part to later.

Keep this in mind: You are not down and out, and you are not soaring too high for the Lord to take you to a new place, a new level. As it is written:

> Do not remember the former things, nor consider the things of old. Behold, I will do a new thing, now it shall spring forth; shall you not know it? I will even make a road in the wilderness and rivers in the desert (Isaiah 43:18-19).

The Lord is about to do a new thing. Resources will flood in from the north, the south, the east, and the west. They are about to flow in unprecedented ways; watch for them. Be ready and do not judge. The Lord's ways are not our ways, nor are His thoughts our thoughts. Have you ever thought what you would do if a mafia boss or cartel head came to you, got saved, and said, "Here is a hundred million dollars. Use it for the body of Christ." What about if a distillery owner offered the same amount? Some would not take it; it would seem wrong to them—but money in itself is not evil, nor can it be. It is *the love* of money that is the root of all evil. Money in itself is a tool to get the job done.

> For the love of money [that is, the greedy desire for it and the willingness to gain it unethically] is a root of all sorts of evil, and some by longing for it have wandered away from the faith and pierced themselves [through and through] with many sorrows (1 Timothy 6:10 AMP).

We are about to see this new thing, and it is going to be amazing, leaving us in wonder when we see the signs and miracles and the financial harvests pouring in from everywhere in such an abundance that no man will be able to say, "Look! I did this with my own hands." God has not, will not, nor ever will, share His glory.

Lastly, we are going to be at the right place at the right time and people are going to sow into the vision the Lord has given us.

> Write the vision and make it plain on tablets, that he may
> run who reads it (Habakkuk 2:2).

The Lord will cause people to see your vision and sow into it. This applies to all kinds of people: Christian men and women, people in the marketplace (saved and unsaved alike), even the wealth of the Gentiles will be transferred when we are kingdom-focused. When it is all about the kingdom of God, He will move on people. Press in and watch and see what the Lord will do. Arise, shine; for your light has come!

What if we all could believe for the transfer of the wealth of the Gentiles to the hands of the righteous? *What if we all could pray for it* to be transferred so the kingdom could and would be expanded? *What if we all prayed that the Lord would raise up those who are all called* to this ministry, and that the provision to reap this end-time harvest would come in? *What if* instead of tearing down these people, *we would build these entrepreneurs of God up*? *What if* we encouraged them and supported them so they could fulfill their destinies? They are called to extreme living. They are called to spend hours upon hours in the presence of the Lord to receive these inspirations, inventions, strategies, and the like. They are also called to extreme giving for the expansion of the kingdom. Will they be blessed? Absolutely. However, they will also have a great understanding that this is not about them or their kingdom; It is about Him and His kingdom. It is for Jesus. If they can't go, they will send people into the harvest field.

If you know you have been called to this, *Do not give up!* It is coming and soon. *The return of Jesus is imminent, and the provision to reap the harvest needs to come in.* Keep believing, keep seeking, and keep soaking in Him! It is all about to break forth to the glory of the Lord. I am waiting for more witty ideas. The Lord has shown me different things, and I know it is all about to happen. He gave me a beautiful wife who truly understands the call of God upon her life and the fullness of it, and that she is called to walk with me in this. She wants to harness the entrepreneurial giftings upon her life. I waited a lifetime for someone to walk with me, so we could reap the harvest set before us. I thank God for Angie every day, so I encourage you this way: If you are reading this and it resonates with your spirit, ask the Lord to use you as an end-time sower. He is always looking for people who will give with a generous heart. If He can use Angie and I, He can use you. He is a good God. Become an extreme giver and live an extreme life!

Chapter Six: Know Your Place

In 2008 I was the Victoria State President for Chariots of Light Motorcycle Ministries, which is part of Jerry Savelle Ministries. This is a powerful ministry in the United States. They do outstanding outreaches into the biker scene. For instance, they go to Sturgis, South Dakota every year, set up a tent, and preach the gospel. It is a ten-day event, and they get there early before it begins and leave long after it is finished. More than 500,000 people attend this event, and every year they see fruit. Hundreds, if not thousands, get saved, and even more receive ministry. They pray for thousands and thousands of bikers over the two-week period, and it is wonderful. Every year they go back and are welcomed with open arms (even now). What a ministry!

In 2007 I received a phone call from a friend of mine named Darren. I met him a year or so earlier at the Christian Outreach Center in Brisbane, Australia. At the time, Darren was the secretary for the Tribe of Judah Motorcycle Ministries. I shared the vision the Lord had put on my heart for a motorcycle ministry, and he called and said, "John, the Lord told me to call you. I am now the Australian National President for Chariots of Light. I believe the Lord said you are to be the Victorian State President." At the time I was living in Melbourne, Victoria, and I thought, *Awesome!* I'm not sure if it was my spirit or my flesh that leaped. Therefore I said to him, "Mate, my flesh is all over this. I'm going to pray about this and when the Holy Spirit tells me I am in, then I am in. But if He says no, I'm not. I'll give you a call when I have heard from the Lord."

So I prayed; and man, did I pray! I prayed every day, seeking His will because, like I said, my flesh was all-in and I had to be sure it was really

God. Two weeks later, Darren called and asked if I was going to do it. I had to tell him that I hadn't heard anything from God yet. Once again I told him I would call him when I had heard from the Lord—either way. Two days later, the Holy Spirit spoke to me, saying He wanted me to take the position. I immediately called Darren. I was so excited! *I was in!* Both of us were excited. When I got off the phone, my first wife said, "How are you going to start a motorcycle ministry with no bike?" (That was the voice of the dream killer.) I looked at her and said, "The Lord told me to do the possible and He would do the impossible." I went to Pastor Graham and shared this with him. He was enthusiastic, and agreed that it was one hundred percent God. He got completely behind it and pushed it. There's nothing better than having your senior pastor support your vision and totally endorse it. He even gave me an office in the church to run the club. For the next month I did all I could do (the possible). Between Darren and I, we rewrote the rules, regulations, and vision for the group to suit Australian culture. We put everything in place. At this point, the Lord was drawing people who felt called to the ministry. It was just happening.

As I did all I was told to do, I went to the Lord and said, "Lord, I kinda need a bike now." The Holy Spirit said, "Set a launch date." I went to Pastor Graham and we set a date; we would launch in thirty days. About two weeks later Pastor Graham and I went for lunch. (That's one of our things: We both love restaurants and good food.) While eating, I really felt we were to go look at Harleys. We went to the first shop, but there was nothing for me there. We went to the second, and still nothing, so we went on to the third. Again, nothing, but I knew the salesperson there. We were about to walk out and he asked me what I was looking for. I told him I wanted a black '95 to '99 Harley Fatboy (an Evo), and it had to have this and that, plus low mileage, and that I only wanted to spend about $20,000. (Bear in mind that this was all by faith. I had no money!) The guy said he did not have anything like that. As we turned to walk out, he called after us, "Wait a minute! Come out to the workshop. I just took a trade-in late last night, and it hasn't even hit the showroom yet." So the pastor and I walked into the workshop, and there it was: Everything I had just asked for was sitting on a stand, ready to be serviced. Pastor Graham looked at me and started laughing. It was amazing! Then the guy asked, "Well, what do you want to do?" The pastor answered for me, "Wow! I can't believe we found a '99 Fatboy! I am going to put a $1,000 on my credit card to hold it. This is the Lord. We will sort it out later."

By faith I had a bike! Now all I needed was twenty-odd grand to take it home. Another week passed and we were getting closer to the launch date. I was seeking the Lord: pressing in and praising Him, knowing He was about to make a way where there seemed to be no way. (In fact, this process continues in my life today. As I am writing, Angie and I are believing for something that's really big—actually, it's the biggest thing yet. It has stirred our faith to really press in with everything we've got. Maybe you are believing for something too. And here's the deal: If it's God, it will happen. But let's get back to my story.) One week before our launch, someone in church gave me a check for $50,000. A couple of days later, the same person drove me up to the motorcycle shop to pick up my bike. Is God good or what? He gets you saved, cleans you up, puts you on a Harley, and sends you out preaching. It doesn't get any better than that!

Pastor Graham had set aside a whole weekend for the launch, and Darren had contacted Jerry Savelle Ministries, telling them we were having a Chariots weekend and launch. They, in turn, sent Reverend Joe as our guest speaker. What an awesome man of God! The whole weekend was great! By this time we had sixteen patched members (and the chapter grew to about thirty plus.) We had a bike run, and the Lord told me to let brother Joe use my Harley (I had had it for a week); and I rode a Suzuki instead. (Hmm, I repented later.) Sunday came and Joe spoke. The word he brought was so incredible that I am going to share some of it here for you too:

Joe spoke on "knowing your place" and walking in it. Joe is a man who knows his place. He is Jerry Savelle's cousin and also his right-hand man, so he is the international director for Jerry Savelle Ministries. Joe shared that second place to Brother Jerry was his *first place in God,* and that this is where the Lord had placed him and where he was supposed to be. Joe explained that we needed to be where the Lord wanted us to be. He said that many opportunities had arisen over the years for him to go out on his own and have his own ministry, but he knew that the Lord had placed him with Brother Jerry and he was being faithful to God in that calling. Brother Joe has traveled the world, preaching the gospel and being used by the Lord everywhere he goes. His revelation that *first place is second place* was truly outstanding, and ministered to many people. Brother Joe is a blessed man on so many levels.

At the time I heard this, we were a church of about six or seven hundred (or more). Everyone who heard that word was blown away by that. The Lord had spoken to me, telling me to take the position of Victorian State President. As people were coming into the club, there were some who came in with their own agenda. It was amazing to watch people. The ones with agendas came in looking for positions for whatever reason. Some wanted to be Victorian State president or vice president or whatever, but not simply a warrior for Christ without a title. At the launch, some came just to hear Brother Joe. When we go to church because we want to hear a word, God shows up and speaks to us.

My point in this is that we all need to be where Lord has called us to be, doing what God has called us to do to fulfill His purpose for us, so that later we can hear, "Well done, good and faithful servant, enter into My rest."

> His lord said to him, "Well done, good and faithful servant; you were faithful over a few things, I will make you ruler over many things. Enter into the joy of your lord" (Matthew 25:21).

We are not to covet what others have. We are to rejoice in what the Lord has given us. Each and every one of us is unique, created by God with a special part to play or role to fulfill. We are the body of Christ, and each a separate member of that body. Without the other parts, we would cease to exist. Can a body function without a heart? You can have a heart, but with no brain, how would it work? So it is vital to our growth and the health of the church that we find our place in the Lord and hear from Him. Brother Joe was reaching his potential and fulfilling his calling in the Lord in the position he had, and he was content.

> From Him the whole body [the church, in all its various parts], joined and knitted firmly together by what every joint supplies, when each part is working properly, causes the body to grow and mature, building itself up in [unselfish] love (Ephesians 4:16 AMP).

This sums it up perfectly:

> If the foot says, "Because I am not a hand, I am not a part of the body," is it not on the contrary still a part of the body? If the ear says, "Because I am not an eye, I am not a part of the body," is it not on the contrary still a part of the body? If the whole body were an eye, where would the hearing be? If the whole [body] were an ear, where would the sense of smell be? But now [as things really are], God has placed and arranged the parts in the body, each one of them, just as He willed and saw fit [with the best balance of function]. If they all were a single organ, where would [the rest of] the body be? But now [as things really are] there are many parts [different limbs and organs], but a single body. The eye cannot say to the hand, "I have no need of you," nor again the head to the feet, "I have no need of you." But quite the contrary, the parts of the body that seem to be weaker are [absolutely] necessary; and as for those parts of the body which we consider less honorable, these we treat with greater honor; and our less presentable parts are treated with greater modesty, while our more presentable parts do not require it. But God has combined the [whole] body, giving greater honor to that part which lacks it, so that there would be no division or discord in the body [that is, lack of adaptation of the parts to each other], but that the parts may have the same concern for one

another. And if one member suffers, all the parts share the suffering; if one member is honored, all rejoice with it (1 Corinthians 12:15-26 AMP).

We all need to find our place in the body of Christ and do whatever we are called to do to the glory of the Lord. Finding your destiny is incredibly important. So is trusting God with it. *What if* your destiny, the only thing you ever did, was to lead the next Billy Graham (or a person of that caliber) to the Lord? And then he (or she) went on to bring thirty-five million plus souls into the kingdom? Those souls would be credited to you as well! If that was all that the Lord ever asked of that person, He would say, "Well done, good and faithful servant, enter into the joy of your Lord!" Not all of us are called to stand before thousands, *but we are all called to do something.* If you're not sure what that is, just *ask Him and then wait.* The Word says that the Holy Spirit will bring us into all truth and tell us of things to come. Ask Him. *He will answer.*

We all need to be ready for the glory that is about to be released upon the earth. We need to live so close to the Lord that when He speaks, we respond with a yes right away. We need to move in obedience to the Holy Spirit. When you think about it, a life could depend on it.

Death and life are in the power of the tongue, and those who love it will eat its fruit (Proverbs 18:21).

Ironically, I have often heard this verse used with a negative focus. While it is true that if you speak negative things, you will reap that, the reverse is also true: If you speak positive things, you reap positive. We can speak in faith…or not. It is our choice. There is another verse that flows with this one:

I charge you therefore before God and the Lord Jesus Christ, who will judge the living and the dead at His appearing and His kingdom: Preach the word! Be ready in season and out of season. Convince, rebuke, exhort, with all longsuffering and teaching (2 Timothy 4:1-2).

Death and life *are* in the power of the tongue! We are to preach the Word and be ready in season *and* out of season, which is literally all the time! We are to convince, rebuke, and exhort, with all longsuffering and teaching.

Some time ago, I was at a Christian business lunch in Melbourne. I had been going there for at least a couple years at this point. David and May Wan would open their boardroom every Wednesday, provide a Chinese buffet for sixty to one hundred and twenty people, and host guest ministers from all over the world. David and May Wan had no agendas, no ulterior motives, but just wanted to serve the Lord with everything they had. (Amazingly, they're lawyers! Just joking.) On this particular day, we had just finished lunch and the praise and worship was about to start, when May Wan came to me and asked if I would share my testimony right before the main speaker from Malaysia came up. I answered with that verse: "Yes, the Word says to always be ready—in season and out. I am ready."

I had shared my testimony many times before, but on this day I truly was not ready. I stopped and asked the Holy Spirit what I should share. One of the advantages to having a colorful past like mine is that there is a lot to share. What I share changes according to the people hearing me to some degree. At the right time, I went to the front and stood there for a minute, praying inwardly what I always prayed: *Holy Spirit, what do You want me to say today?* Sounds simple, doesn't it? But what He answered was not what I expected, and it was something I never wanted to share. He told me to start from the beginning, and I said, *No, Lord!* The Holy Spirit repeated Himself: *John, from the beginning.* Again I said, *No, Lord, I can't.* Again, He responded with, *John, from the beginning.* I said, *Lord, I have never shared this.* And of course, God knew that. In actual fact, I had only ever shared it with my first wife (and we had been married for years before I even told her)! Have you ever had an argument with the Lord in your head? It seemed like it went on forever, and I felt my face getting red under the pressure. Picture it! Here is this evangelist who can talk underwater, standing like a statue in front of this huge group of people and saying nothing at all, while he just gets redder and redder. I was in freeze-frame. May Wan was staring, and I imagined she was thinking, *Well, anytime now, John!* (At least, that thought entered *my* mind). The argument ensued, and the Holy Spirit stood firm, *John, from the beginning!*

I opened my mouth, and for the very first time, I shared about how I had been sexually abused as a child. I had been three or four years old and was taken down the hallway to the bathroom by a babysitter in my yellow cowboy and Indian pajamas. As I spoke, I felt ashamed and embarrassed and humiliated all over again; and then, something lifted off me. Standing before roughly 100 people (or so) who had never heard my testimony, *I was instantly delivered of all of it*. To this point I had always shared about my life with drugs, alcohol, sex, and crime, but had never shared why I went that way. I went on to say that because of the abuse, I was a very angry kid by the time I was seven or eight. I hated all authority, and I mean all authority: teachers, police, bosses, even my parents at times. (And I had great parents and I love them. They never knew about the abuse. I told my mom about it after this meeting, but my dad had already passed away by this time. I honor my mom and dad. This was never about them. It was about authority and what had happened to me.)

So back to the meeting. I was sharing that driven by my anger, I began smoking dope and dealing drugs when I was thirteen. Then I began drinking. My smoking and drinking went on almost daily for twenty plus years. Daily depression and suicidal thoughts occurred throughout that time. I shared a lot more, but what happened later was just astounding to me. The Asian speaker got up and shared next. When it was over, everyone was getting ready to leave, and out of this crowd of business people came this guy who really didn't even look like he fit in. Everyone else was dressed in preppy casual or business attire, but this guy was wearing an old T-shirt, jeans and sneakers. I had never seen him before nor since. He looked at me and said, "Hey, you need to know something. I was going home to commit suicide today, but because of your story and what you went through, I know I can make it through this too." I thought, *Wow, thank You, Lord!* I was just about to ask what part of my testimony spoke to him, as it was the first time I had ever shared that, when the Holy Spirit spoke very clearly: *Be quiet. Not a word. It is none of your business.* I said, *What, Lord?* Again I heard, *It is none of your business.* I thought, *Wow!* (I have had a lot of "wow" moments with the Lord). The guy looked at me and said, "Thanks," shook my hand, and walked away.

It is absolutely true! Death and life are in the power of the tongue. We are to preach the Word! Be ready in season and out of season. Convince, rebuke, exhort, with all longsuffering and teaching.

This was mind-blowing to me. Not only do we need to watch what we say, but *we need to be mindful to say the things led by the Holy Spirit.* What if I had not done as the Holy Spirit directed me? This guy could have gone home and killed himself!

We need to know who we are in Christ, and we need to know our authority in Him. We need to know our place with—and through—Him. We all have a place and a call, and we are all members of His body: every one of us, no matter how insignificant we may feel that we are. The Father of all creation has created you for a particular position, and *nobody else can do it.* We need to understand that God the Father, our Abba, loves each and every one of us the same. Abba has no favorites. In love, we are all created equal. He loves us the same, no matter what. Creed, color, race? Daddy doesn't see any of that. Social and economic stature mean nothing to Him; geographic position and descendants mean nothing to the Lord. His love is unconditional. Do you understand that? There are absolutely no conditions to His love. He wants you exactly the way you are. His love is so great that He will never leave you where you are, but will take you from glory to glory. That is His promise.

Press in, and seek the Lord with everything you have. There is just so much more in Him. He is waiting for us to press in, so He can reveal Himself to us. Abba wants to pour His glory upon us all. Jesus says He stands at the door, waiting. There is nothing more marvelous than sitting and having coffee with the Lord in the morning. As we do this, the Holy Spirit starts pouring His love and glory upon us. The presence of the

Lord is tangible, even weighty, and precious. So we say, "Lord, if this is all I can have, this is enough." *But it's not!* He has so much more. We cannot comprehend the fullness of His glory. Every day, Angie and I pray, "More, Lord; we must decrease that You may increase. Lord, show us Your glory, just as You did for Moses. Take us deeper in You!" Every day we enter in, expecting more than the day before, *and He shows up every day without fail.* We sit and bask in Him, spending two, three, and four hours a morning with Him, just worshiping, praising and soaking, praying, and waiting on Him. This is for everyone.

John, I work. Yeah, I understand. For years I got up at five o'clock so I could have a minimum of three hours with the Holy Spirit. Then I went to work at nine. I did this because the Holy Spirit said to me, "Blessed is the man who rises early to seek the Lord." I thought, *That's good!* I began to get up at five at that time. I didn't need an alarm clock because He woke me every morning. I made my coffee, sat down, and started my morning by saying, "Good morning, Holy Spirit!" I still do all these years later. I read Benny Hinn's book called *Good Morning, Holy Spirit* and thought, *What a great way to start the day!* If you haven't read that book, it is an awesome read. Once I wanted to preach about what the Lord said to me, but could not find those exact words anywhere in the Bible. But the concept is there in many places:

> I rise before dawn and cry for help; I wait for Your words.
> (Psalm 119:147 NASB).

The Lord wants to commune with us. He wakes me at five every morning because He wants to spend time with me. Isn't that incredibly neat? And I am not somehow special. *He wants this with everyone.* This is how much He loves us.

All in all, I know that knowing who you are in Christ, knowing your authority, knowing your place, and exercising it will bring you into a greater dimension with the Lord. Our God loves us, and He loves the world. Through a greater level of intimacy, we will be able to love as the Father loves, and we will see the greatest revival ever seen by man. Press in! His glory is for everyone who asks. He will not withhold from anyone who seeks Him. If you feel led, please pray this prayer with me for a greater level of intimacy:

> *Father, I come to You. In Jesus' name, I want a deeper, purer walk with You. I want to experience a greater level of intimacy. Holy Spirit, draw me unto You in a new and greater way. I surrender all to You afresh today. Holy Spirit, search my heart; if there is anything in there that is not of You, I give You permission to bring it to the surface so it can go. Lord, I only want Your Spirit and my spirit. Everything else has to go. Holy Spirit, I ask You to release Your glory upon me so I may be closer to You. I only want to walk in my place, the one you have ordained for me before I was even born. If I am not walking in my place or Your perfect will, please show me. My heart is to be where You want me, doing what You have called me to do. I love You, Lord, and I ask for more of You, in Jesus' name, Amen.*

So what if we could all find our place and be content in it? What if second place was your first place? *What if* first place was your first place? As long as we are doing what we are called to do (and we are all called somehow), that is enough! We must be in the right place at the right time, doing the things we are called to do. We are never to covet another person's position, nor are we to work off another man's foundation (trying to take it over or conspiring against him). Each and every one of us is called to our own ministry, even if it is working with, or for, another ministry. Take Brother Joe, for example. His place is second place to Brother Jerry, and he serves Brother Jerry and his ministry wholeheartedly. However, the Lord has used Brother Joe around the whole world in doing that; he preaches and reaps a harvest all the time. Brother Joe is fulfilling his ministry within another ministry, but everything is unto the Lord. Now that is *extreme living*, knowing your place and fulfilling your destiny, no matter what it is and doing it all for God. May we all come to a knowledge of knowing our place and living in it to God's glory.

Chapter Seven: Why Am I Here?

Like Joseph, at an early age I knew something others didn't. I don't know how and I didn't know why, but I knew that I knew. I knew I was put here to do something great, but had no idea what. I just knew. The first time I ever shared this with anyone, I was laughed at. Picture this: I was fourteen and sitting on the bank of the hospital hill in Kitimat, British Columbia, in Canada where I was born. I was with two of my buddies, smoking a joint or two. I looked over to them and said, "You know, I've been put on this earth to do something great!" They just laughed. One of them said, "We are in Kitimat! What could you do from here?" Kitimat is so far north of Vancouver that it is actually only five hours south of Hyder, Alaska. It is in the middle of nowhere. At that time, it had a population of about 9,000 people. These friends could not imagine anything good that could come out of Kitimat; and quite frankly, out of me. I was just a funny guy who smoked a lot of weed and drank a lot. Seriously, what could I do? Thinking of that is amazing to me today, though. Hindsight is an awesome teacher.

For many years I never knew why I felt this. I just did. It wasn't until the Lord had me move from Hervey Bay, Queensland, Australia, back to Melbourne, also in Australia, about seven years ago. I climbed off the plane, was picked up, and taken straight to a conference that was about to begin. The conference was at Pastor Graham's church, the I AM House Of Worship in Hoppers Crossing, a suburb of Melbourne. The guest speaker was Pastor Judith. She moved in the glory of God like no one I had ever seen before then. The manifestations of the Spirit through her were amazing. She was praying for people and people were literally being taken to heaven in the Spirit and having amazing encounters. I was just standing there in awe, maybe even in wonder. An old guy with lung cancer was healed (this was documented), and many other signs and miracles occurred. She called me out and said, "The Lord wants you to come up!"

> After these things I looked, and behold, a door standing open in heaven. And the first voice which I heard was like a trumpet speaking with me, saying, "Come up here, and I will show you things which must take place after this" (Revelation 4:1).

I was more a little skeptical, but went up. She prayed for me, and I was slain in the Spirit. As I lay on the floor, I felt my spirit man rising out of my body, which really freaked me out. I could literally feel it rising up. I panicked and thought, *Wow, I don't know if I'm ready to stand before the Lord!* Then I felt my spirit man lower and come back into my body. I got up, and Pastor Judith called me again, saying, "John, the Lord wants you to come up! He has things He wants to show you." She prayed for me, and bam, I was back on the floor and I felt my spirit man rising up again. Once again, I panicked. This was all new to me, and my thought was still, *I don't know if I am ready to see Jesus!* Immediately, I felt my spirit lower back into my body and again got up. Judith prayed over me again, and the same thing happened for the third time. As I felt my spirit lifting out of my body this time, I thought, *Lord, I have done so many bad things in my life. I don't think I am worthy to come up.* With that, I felt my spirit enter back into my body; I got up and felt disappointed. Judith called me again, and started praying. Then the Holy Spirit took over and He spoke through her. He said, "John, come up, come up! You have been up here many times before!" Suddenly I had a flashback of my youth (I will get to that in a second). Judith prayed for me again, and this time when I hit the deck, I was gone. I found myself in heaven. I was in the banquet room. I don't know how I knew that, but I knew.

It was amazing! There was a table as far as the eye could see, set and adorned with the most incredible things. No earthly royalty had anything like it. I was awestruck as I realized where I was. I thought, *Wow! I am in the banquet room! I made it! I am actually standing in the banquet room!* This realization that my sins had been forgiven truly overwhelmed me. I just stared at this massive table: so wide, so long, covered with beautiful ornaments, plates, cutlery, sensational wine glasses, and finely-wrought tablecloths. Even the chairs were spectacular. As I was looking with wonder at the table, it turned into a massive conveyor belt. A long way away, I could see something coming up the conveyor. I could make out different-sized objects. As they got closer, I could see they were boxes of all shapes and sizes, and each one was wrapped, beautifully wrapped. I thought, *What is this?* A voice answered clearly (but not audibly), *These are the gifts that I have for you.* Strangely enough, I didn't talk, nor did anyone else. You just knew what was going on (it is hard to explain). I was completely overwhelmed. When I got up, I was asked to share what I saw, and I did. I told everyone, "Man, I was in the banquet room, my sins have truly been forgiven, and I am washed in the blood. He who the Son sets free is free indeed." Then I stood and praised God. Immediately I was back in Kitimat in my mind.

What Pastor Judith had said came flooding back to me: "Come up, you have been up here many times before!" I said, *Lord, when?* And suddenly it came back to me. When I was about ten years old and I would go to bed (and I am not sure if I was asleep or just about asleep), my body would start twirling. I would feel my spirit lifting out of my body, but at that time I didn't know what was happening. It would spin like a whirlwind and up I would go. I do not know how many times this happened, but it was often. It happened enough that I told my mom about it. After quite a few occurrences, she took me to the doctor, thinking maybe something was wrong with me. This kind-of scared me, so as I prayed about it and asked the Lord to show me if it was real. I asked Him to show me in the Bible (as we were taught that everything had to line up with the Word).

> And it came to pass, when the Lord was about to take up Elijah into heaven by a whirlwind…Then it happened, as they continued on and talked, that suddenly a chariot of

fire appeared with horses of fire, and separated the two of them; and Elijah went up by a whirlwind into heaven (2 Kings 2:1, 11).

And

Then the Lord answered Job out of the whirlwind, and said: (Job 38:1).

So all the days of Enoch were three hundred and sixty-five years. And Enoch walked with God; and he was not, for God took him (Genesis 5:23-24).

There are twenty-two different references to a whirlwind in the Bible. I was only ten and I was taken up into heaven. I have been there many times since, yet I have not seen the same things others have seen. It is truly a wonderful place!

So here I was, believing I had been put on the earth for something special, but what good could come out of Kitimat? What good could come out of me? I was damaged goods, and didn't even know that. (I thought everyone else had the problems.) At school I was a bully because of all the hurt and anger inside me. (I didn't understand this then, but I do now.) My buddies and I used to sit at the front doors of the school, and I ridiculed just about everyone who walked in. My friends thought it was funny and laughed. (After I was born again, I often thought about the hurt and pain I must have caused others. My actions were unkind, unnecessary, and just plain wrong. I know Jesus has forgiven me, but if you are reading this and you were one of the many I verbally abused, I ask for your forgiveness too. I am sorry for acting as I did. Please forgive me. There was no excuse for it.)

Why am I here today? I shouldn't be! I should be dead! I am here by the grace of God. I know that God preserved my life, and in truth, He does that for all of us.

One Friday night we were out drinking and smoking dope, and for whatever reason, a friend and I thought it would be good to do some car surfing; this was in 1977. Here we were in another friend's Nova. It was primed for paint, so it was quite gritty. We are cruising down the highway on the hood, going about 100 kilometers (about 62 miles per hour). All in all, it seemed like good fun. A couple days later, we were telling a different friend about it, so he said, "Let's try it on my car." Everyone piled in, with me on the hood holding a football in one hand and the windshield wiper arm in the other. We took off, and as he sped up, I started slipping. (His car had just come out of the body shop, so it had fresh paint.) I yelled, "Hey, dude, I'm slipping." We were whipping by the school, and people were watching everywhere. He thought I was joking, and hammered it. At this point, we were going about eighty kilometers (50 mph), and I flew off the car. My head smashed off the concrete, and then bounced a few times as I went sliding down the road on my shoulder. My friend stopped, and everyone in the car still thought it was all pretty funny. I regained consciousness and stood up, and one of my friends told me to pick up the football that was on the ground. As I bent over to pick it up, I passed out—and that's all I remember.

A few of them picked me up off the road and carried me to the grass. When I woke, a lot of the hair on my head had come out, and my knuckles, wrist, and elbow had a lot of the flesh scraped off. Onlookers who had seen the whole thing said they were amazed that I had not fallen under the car or that I hadn't been killed from cracking my head on the concrete. They expected me to have major injuries, or even end up in a wheelchair. This was the first of many near-death experiences. I was sharp all right: sharp like a marble.

On another occasion, I was delivering furniture for a store; it was my teenage part-time job. I had to deliver some furniture to Thornlands out near Terrace, about 50 kms away from Kitimat. I asked my friend Brian if he wanted to come along for the drive, so we went out, did the job, and were heading home. The sun was going down and we were on a straight stretch. It was a good road and the sun was behind us; but for oncoming traffic, the sun would have been right in front and blinding. There was a car coming toward us and a big, four-wheel drive vehicle behind it. We were just coming up to the first vehicle when I saw the bigger vehicle pull out to pass the first car. The sun had to have been blinding him; I could not see well with the glare bouncing back at me either. I looked to the passenger side, but there was little space there. It was a sheer drop on my friend's side. It went straight down, and there was absolutely no room for three-cars wide. If I steered wrong, we were toast, and if I didn't move, we were dead for sure. We are going 100 km (60 mph) and I knew the passing vehicle had to be going faster. I also knew he didn't see us. With only a car length between us, I swerved right. As I did, I saw the other vehicle miss the back of our van by an inch, if that. I was trying to keep the van from going over the edge, but it all happened in seconds. It all felt like slow motion. I got the van back on the road and found a place to pull over. My heart was in my throat. Brian was speechless. He finally looked at me and said, "I thought we were going to die! Good driving!" At that time, I didn't know God, but now I know that it wasn't me—now I know about grace and angels. Even now as I revisit it in my mind, I know that there wasn't room for three vehicles at that speed on that road. We didn't speak a lot for the rest of the trip. We both knew we should have been dead. Neither of us questioned why we weren't; we just knew we should have been. Angels? I don't know. It was simply miraculous, and that is all I knew. The reason I am sharing this is to prove a point: All our books are written in heaven, and Daddy knows our every day. He will preserve us to fulfill those days He has planned for us. Again Psalm 139 says:

> Your eyes saw my substance, being yet unformed. And in
> Your book they all were written, the days fashioned for
> me, when as yet there were none of them (Psalm 139:16).

We all go through things—but we all need to come out the other side. God has a purpose for each and every one of us. Why do some people go through more than others? I bet you thought I would have the answer. Nope. I don't know. I do know that everything we go through has a reason behind it. I am still alive today. Why? Because God kept me alive.

Something happened to the friend of mine from the last story that transformed his life. Sometime after that incident, we just partied harder and harder. One day we are at Brian's house (well, his mom's), and we were partying, as we did just about every Friday and Saturday night before his mom got home from work. On this day my friend had scored some black hash that was laced with opium. He had a block of it, and as always, we started smoking and drinking, just getting ready to go out. We got wasted and left his house just before his mom got home. He and some other dudes went their way, and I went with some other friends and did our thing. About a week or so later, I said to my friend's brother, "Where has Brian been? I haven't seen him all week!" He said, "Me neither." When Friday came around again, I was smoking and drinking again. There were about ten of us there, and in came Brian. He spoke to me, saying, "Hey, John, can I talk to you?" I said, "Go ahead, talk." He looked at me and said, "No, in private, in the bedroom." I'm thinking, *This is weird.*

Off we went to the bedroom. He asked me to sit down. So here I am in a bedroom with a guy who wants to have a heart-to-heart. I just wanted to say, "You're killing me here, dude," but I said nothing. Brian began by asking me if I remembered last week when we were smoking hash, and I said that I did. He went on to tell me that he overdosed and ended up in the hospital. I was looking at him, thinking, *Wow, this is heavy.* Then he said, "But that isn't the weird bit. I saw Jesus." I said, "What do you mean, you saw Jesus?" He said, "Jesus showed up in my hospital room!" I looked at him and asked, "Why are you telling me this?" He said he had to tell someone. I said, "Why me?" (Beyond that, I was speechless.) Brian answered with a question: "Why do you think?" Not knowing what to say and being more than a little freaked out, I said, "Hey, man, where can I get some more of that hash?" It amazed me. After that, I watched Brian's life transform. I sat back and just watched how things were changing. Brian met this intense dude named Tom at his work. Tom really freaked me out. Here was this massive guy, telling me I needed Jesus, I went to his house for about a week to listen to him with my friend. The last day I went, he was taking me through the book of Revelation. I wasn't even saved yet. He was telling me about the end times. There was a newspaper on his table. I picked it up and said, "Between the things you are telling me and what this newspaper says, I have lots of time. No thank you!" And I left. How foolish! I had no understanding that at any time, my life could be required by God. I didn't realize that I would stand before the Lord someday and have to account for my unrepentant sin, as well as for denying Jesus as my Savior. I closed my eyes then, but that was when the seed was planted. I went back to partying, girls, drinking, drugs, and selling.

A couple years later, I had another near-death experience. I was living in a small town called White Rock, just south of Vancouver, a border town with the United States. Three of us were out in a friend's boat, and we were drinking. We had about four dozen beers between us. We were about halfway in and cruising the pier, and we saw another friend with his girlfriend and some other good-looking girls. My friend thought he would show off and we started "shooting the pier," meaning that we would maneuver the boat through the gap in the pier's concrete support posts at a fast speed—a very dangerous feat. This was in a no-wake zone, so we would go screaming fast under the pier, then we'd go out a ways, come back in, and shoot the pier again. We did that four or five times, and then stopped while the one guy spoke to his friend on the pier. Some dude who was living on his boat got kind-of mad. I guess we were rocking his boat with the waves, and he started yelling at us. My friend thought this was funny, so he fired up his boat and we went out again and came flying back in and shot the pier again. My friend turned the boat, but we had not gone out far enough, so when we came screaming in again, there was a bang—a huge bang. My body flew from one side of the boat to the other and the small of my back caught the edge of the boat, which prevented my head from smashing against the concrete pylon. It took a bit for me to reach down the side to check the boat; it was split all down the seam. I told my friend about the damage, and we left the area quickly.

We took the boat to the American side. The plan was to say we hit a log or a deadhead and the boat had sunk. Then my friend could collect the insurance. We were about 200 yards from the shore in Blaine, Washington, when someone came up with the awesome idea that since the boat wasn't taking on water very fast, we could just drink the rest of the beer and swim in. Good idea, right? Well, the tide was going out, so here we are, laughing and joking, not noticing a thing. The beer was almost gone, and by now, the boat had heaps of water in it and the motor wouldn't start. We looked and we were extremely far from the shore. It was getting dark, and now we had to swim to shore. I guess this would be a good time to note that there was only one life jacket, and my friend said, "My boat, my life jacket," so he was wearing it. We swam for about an hour and a half, fighting the tide and getting nowhere. I looked at both of these guys and said, "Just leave me! I can't do this." The other guy looked at me and said, "Keep swimming or I am going punch the _____ out of you." So we kept swimming. It was pitch black now, and even though we could see the bar we drank at in Blaine, it was still far away. We were surrounded by sea lions or seals. On one side, we could hear a woman screaming at her husband because he was drunk and throwing up outside. We started screaming for help. Unknown to us (as sound travels on the water), she heard us and called the Coast Guard. An eternity later, we could see them coming. It took them three hours to find us. I'm not sure how long we were in the water, but when we were rescued, we were told that we would never had made it to shore. The water is very cold off the Washington coastline because of the chilly California current. Between exhaustion and hypothermia, all three of us were done. It was an embarrassing newspaper article.

So when do you stop and think, *Wow, enough is enough?* Apparently not yet. All this happened before I was twenty-four, and there was much more that I haven't mentioned. However, my life was about to get worse. My drug dealing and cocaine abuse seemed to spiral out of control over the next nine years. I felt more suicidal at this point than ever before. I could see no purpose in living anymore. Nearly every day I smoked weed and drank; it was the only way I could get to sleep. Without that, I was constantly tormented with thoughts of suicide and killing people who had screwed me over or accused me of doing things I had never done. It often took me two to three hours just to get to sleep. Many nights I told myself, *empty your head, empty your head* over and over for hours; it was easier to get wasted than be tormented. One thing stopped me from committing suicide. When I was about twelve, my grandmother took me aside and said, "Jack, if you get tattoos, you will go to hell!" (Well, I put that to the test.) But the next thing she said was, "Jack, if you commit suicide, you will go to hell." Every time I was at the point of thinking, *I can't live this hell anymore* (and I had guns, rifles, a sawn-off shotgun, all loaded), I would hear my grandma's voice, *Jack, if you commit suicide, you will go to hell.* That stopped me.

I don't know what that was about either. I don't even know why my grandmother said that to me. I have never heard that she said it to anyone else in the family, but thank God for Grandmas. I struggled with believing there even was a God. If there was a God, how could He let a child be sexually abused? We all know that bad things happen to good people, but most of the time we blame God for things He never did nor wanted to happen. Even in all my confusion, her words echoed in my mind: *Jack, if you commit suicide, you will go to hell.* Have you ever thought you were smarter than God or perhaps that you could outsmart Him? Well, I thought that if I couldn't commit suicide, I would just do drugs; and if I overdosed, well, too bad. Such is life, and I could say that it was an accident. Yep, when you are lost, you are lost—and blind as well. When we used magic (hallucinogenic) mushrooms, everyone would take a gram, but I would take two or three. When we did acid, some would have a hit or two, and I would do six. When we did coke, others did a gram, but I did as much as I could. It was the weirdest thing. I got wasted—and I mean, wasted—but not once did I ever overdose. I did come very, very close a few times, though.

I hate sharing this part of my life because it seems like a million years ago now. But this is my testimony of what Jesus delivered me from. Drug dealing was good until you came up short or something went wrong: driving from one city to another with 200 pounds of weed, having kilos and kilos of pot, hash and oil, bags of mushrooms, a hundred lots of acid, uppers, downers, all the time. Dealing cocaine—some straight from Bolivia, Colombia, and Mexico, and crossing the border with crank (methamphetamine) and weed. Having the cops come to your job, take you away, and threaten you with ten years for conspiracy for importing cocaine from America to Canada. Then losing your job because of it. Or when you are asked to help a guy move, and someone tells you to stay away from him but doesn't tell you why, and three dudes show up with uzies and beat the guy up while you are there. It was a coke deal gone bad and a whole ego and territory thing. What a mess!

Then there's this one: A friend asked for an introduction to one of my sources, and I gave it, but of course it went wrong. After that, my people thought I had been in on the deal. They told me they had guns in the car and this was going to get ugly. They left to give me time to think over what I was going to do. When they came back a little later, the dude sent in his woman to speak to my wife to see if she could talk sense into me and get me to deal with them. They thought my wife might be able to help, but she just looked at this woman, and said, "John can take care of himself." By this point, things were getting pretty heated, and I was done. Finally, I said, "One of three things are going to happen here. One: You guys are going to kill me. Two: I am going to kill all of you, or three: We will all be going to jail. Let's get it on either way, because I had nothing to do with any of this and I ain't paying anything to anyone." When you don't care if you live or die, things are different. The woman went to the car, it was quiet for a few minutes, and then the car started up and they left, and that was the end of that.

There were times when I was selling up a storm and things were going good. Money was coming in, coke flying everywhere. Then, for whatever reason, after selling to all these people and watching them crash and burn, someone offered me a crack pipe at a party. Well, maybe it wasn't a party in the normal sense of the word: It was ten or so crackheads all sitting in a circle, except for the one or two on the carpet looking for rocks that no one ever dropped. It was my first time, and my first thought was, *No, don't do this*, but peer pressure won out. I took that first toke on that pipe. How does that feel? Well, your head rings. I mean, it almost blows your mind, then you have another couple tokes. You pull on it as hard as you can, and hold your breath until you can't. It is awesome, but no ringing this time. Then the fourth one and there it is again: ringing—and I mean ringing. Then you find yourself chasing the ring; and it becomes everything to you. Everything gets put on the back burner, and you're a crackhead. Looking back, I still can't believe I was so stupid as to try it. I really did know better.

Another time a friend asked to use my scales. I told them I didn't lend my scales (because they were very good ones). I told him that I would go with him instead, so I left, intending to be back in a couple of hours, but I came back three *days* later. My friend and I had cut and weighed up a bunch of coke. We started cooking it, thinking we would just have a pipeful each and then leave, but an ounce and a half later (and with little to no sleep) we finally got home. Crazy world.

Shortly after that, there was no more profit. I was selling as much as I was smoking. All of a sudden, I was coming up short and I had a $5,000-a-week crack habit. Oh yeah, I also had a wife and three boys, sitting at home wondering where I was and when I'd be home again. Then I went off it cold turkey: no doctors, no rehab, trying to kick the habit, trying to withdraw, sweating uncontrollably. For six months I had pipe dreams, in which I woke up gasping for air and holding my breath, thinking I was on the pipe and not able to breathe. Then came the mood swings. There are so many stories, but the Lord spared my life for His glory. It was crazy. Many times I was soaring: I was up and then I was down; it was a roller coaster of a life if I ever saw one. When you were up, you could pull up outside a nightclub that had a line of people to get in, and walk right in without waiting. You spent everything in your pocket and came back the next day and paid the bar tab. Everything was fantastic. But when I was down, it wasn't quite so nice. Actually, it was pretty ugly.

In 1983, I took this chick on a date. She was a very pretty woman. I took her to see *Scarface,* and well, that was it for her. All I could see from then on was Al Pacino playing Tony Montana. In the story, Tony goes from this nothing kid in Miami to become the biggest drug kingpin ever. I thought, *That's what I want to be: a drug lord.* Was I a good drug dealer? Kinda, but not to the standard of what I wanted. Was I a Tony Montana? Not even close. Did I have large quantities of money and drugs go through my hands? Yes, over the years. I knew many people too, but one thing stopped me from going down that road, and that was the fact that the only way to get to that level involved killing people. You had to kill people to get the respect you needed to carry it out. They had to be afraid of you. After finding the Lord and repenting of all the stuff the Holy Spirit brought to the surface, I once said to Him, "Well at least I don't have to repent of murder." He told me that if I ever thought about murder in my heart, I had already committed murder. I was convicted instantly and had to repent. Over the years, I had spent hours upon hours (understatement) thinking and even planning how to kill certain individuals. (Fortunately, I was talked out of it). A few years back I was stunned when my mom told me that both my mom's and dad's worst fear was that they would be visiting me in prison someday. They were always worried I would kill someone because of the anger they saw in me. Jesus spoke about this too. He said in Matthew 5:21-22 that if you were angry and held anger in your heart toward another, you would be judged for it. Jesus understood how strong emotions damaged our hearts, and that as we acted upon them, they led to sin. He said the sin was present before the act was committed.

I often think back to the times I sat in Pastor Graham's office after something had happened or someone had screwed me over or ripped me off in some way. I would say, "Man, I want to kill that person!" My pastor had no idea (at the time) that it was not just a figure of speech to me. I was serious! Before I had spoken to him about it, I had already thought about doing it for some time! We laugh about it now, but when I first landed in his church, Pastor Graham had a big job cut out for him. If I could turn back time, would I go down the path of my past again? Absolutely not, not for anything. My wife, Angie, always says, "John, you are who you are today because of the road you traveled. If you had not gone down this path, you would be a different person." You gotta love her! The Lord has blessed her with such wisdom and discernment. She is a mighty woman of God, called for such a time as this, and she is my heart's desire. Scripture says that God works all things for good for those called to His purpose. I am thankful God rescued me and can use what I went through now, but that was not His perfect will for anyone.

The Word says, "God gives you the desires of your heart." Does He?

> Delight yourself also in the Lord, and He shall give you
> the desires of your heart (Psalm 37:4).

I have asked this question from the pulpit, and everyone says yes. You should see their faces drop when I say, "No, He doesn't." I wanted to be a drug kingpin from 1983 (and probably longer) until 1993. It wasn't until I got saved, delivered, and progressively healed, and was drawing unto the Lord, seeking Him and His ways with a changed heart and changed desires that He began to give me my heart's desires. He changed them first to line up with His will, and they are so different than they once were. In reality, they are His desires for my life, not mine. Abba is awesome! Amazingly, He took me as I was, turned my world upside down, then set me on fire for Him, and let me go! Now my heart's desire is to reap a harvest of millions. Instead of building my kingdom, I live for His kingdom.

Revelation 12:11 sums it up perfectly:

> And they overcame him (the Devil) by the blood of
> the Lamb and by the word of their testimony, and they
> did not love their lives to the death (Revelation 12:11,
> addition mine).

It is kind of funny. In the beginning of my walk, I shared my testimony with others because that's all I had: what Jesus did for me. Now I love to speak on His goodness, His love, His grace, His mercy, His lovingkindness, His glory, and the most incredible journey of intimacy one can have with such a loving Father. The deeper you go in God, the more it becomes about Him and not you. My life has never been more fulfilled than when I am sharing the love of the Father, being filled with the Holy Spirit and seeing Him respond to his people following the preaching of the gospel. I love exalting the name above every name: Jesus the Messiah, King of the Jews and the Gentiles. Life is awesome! Angie and I are about to embark on the most extreme path that we have ever been on yet. To God be the glory!

I wrote this chapter to glorify what Jesus has done in my life, and share where I came from. There were some amazing and even fun times, good times, and definitely intense times that I chose not to share because it is not in my heart to glorify that lifestyle. There was a time when I lived in the world for the Devil; but now, because of what Jesus has done for me, I can only live 100% for Him. Some might misunderstand me and think of me as arrogant or prideful, but my goal is simply to live all for Jesus. I have had enough of the world. I am all in. It says: "They did not love their lives to the death." If need be, Lord, I'm with that. It is all for Jesus or nothing. I am here for the glory of the Lord, His plan, His purpose:

> Therefore I say to you, her sins, which are many, are forgiven, for she loved much. But to whom little is forgiven, the same loves little (Luke 7:47).

I am forgiven much, so much is required. My heart is to glorify the Lord with my life—at any cost. I want to show God's love and salvation to a dying world, to reap the harvest that is written in my book in heaven. My goal is to honor Jesus in word and action, and be a doer and not just a hearer of the Word.

> But be doers of the word, and not hearers only, deceiving yourselves. For if anyone is a hearer of the word and not a doer, he is like a man observing his natural face in a mirror; for he observes himself, goes away, and immediately forgets what kind of man he was. But he who looks into the perfect law of liberty and continues in it, and is not a forgetful hearer but a doer of the work, this one will be blessed in what he does (James 1:22-25).

For all intents and purposes, I should never have made it this far. I have proof of this. *But God.* God in His wisdom and authority has chosen me, He has called me for such a time as this to fulfill a destiny. I do not deserve it, and yet here I am, like so many others, and I am here to serve the Lord. I thank the Lord for His unmerited grace and mercy, and I say, "Daddy, send me! Daddy, use me for Your glory; here I am."

> Therefore, if anyone is in Christ, he is a new creation; old things have passed away; behold, all things have become new. Now all things are of God, who has reconciled us to Himself through Jesus Christ, and has given us the ministry of reconciliation, that is, that God was in Christ reconciling the world to Himself, not imputing their trespasses to them, and has committed to us the word of reconciliation. Now then, we are ambassadors for Christ, as though God were pleading through us: we implore you on Christ's behalf, be reconciled to God. For He made Him who knew no sin to be sin for us, that we might become the righteousness of God in Him (2 Corinthians 5:17-21).

I am saved by grace and I'm a new creation in Him; old things have passed away. So why am I here?

> But God has selected [for His purpose] the foolish things of the world to shame the wise [revealing their ignorance], and God has selected [for His purpose] the weak things of the world to shame the things which are strong [revealing their frailty] (1 Corinthians 1:27 AMP).

Other translations say God "confounds the wise" (instead of shames). I have no formal training. I asked the Lord about going to Bible college, and He said, "Did I tell you to go?" I am where I am thirty-two years later through the Holy Spirit's leading. Father God, Jesus, and the Holy Spirit get all the credit and all the glory for everything I have done that turned out well. They have formed me. It's all His doing. He called me and I answered. Have I made mistakes? Yes, and they were mine, not His. I am learning. Show me someone who hasn't made a mistake, and I will show you a liar. There was (and is) only one perfect One: Jesus.

Remember: "It is no longer I that live, but Christ that lives in me." I speak to your spirit man, and say, "Arise, shine for the glory of the Lord is upon you! Grab your vision and run with it. Never, never give up (Winston Churchill said no.). The time is short! Let us all stand before the Lord and hear Him say, 'Well done, good and faithful servant; enter into the joy of the Lord. You ran your race and completed it! Well done!'" Jesus has called everyone for something. If you don't know what it is, then ask, and the Holy Spirit will show you. When you seek Him with all your heart, soul, and mind, He is a faithful God. Everyone has a destiny in Him, and I mean *everyone*.

I should not be here, but I am. Why? Because the Lord has a purpose for me. *What if* the Lord has a purpose for you—and it is so far out there that it seems daunting, even unattainable? *What if* you said, "Yes, Lord here am I, I can't do this on my own, but I am here for You to use as You have planned. Use me, Lord"? Someone reading this could say, "I have done so many bad things, I can't be forgiven!" or "John, I would like to believe this, but…so many things!" To that I say: If you truly come before the Lord from you heart and ask Jesus to come into your life and ask Him to take it over, *He will*. If you ask Him to forgive you of all you have done, *He will*. He forgave Paul (Saul) who persecuted and killed Christians! Paul lived an amazing life for Jesus after he repented and was transformed.

What if the extreme life you led for the Devil was gone, but the Lord cleaned you up and you then led an extreme life for Him instead? *What if* you have been saved for years and you have just never picked up the ball and ran with it? I'm sharing this with you to say this: God has a purpose and a destiny for everyone. If you are not walking in it, then it's time to pick up that ball. *Extreme living is wonderful. There's nothing better!*

Chapter Eight: Intimacy: Deep Calling unto Deep

O Lord, you have searched me [thoroughly] and have known me. You know when I sit down and when I rise up [my entire life, everything I do]; You understand my thought from afar. You scrutinize my path and my lying down, and You are intimately acquainted with all my ways. Even before there is a word on my tongue [still unspoken], behold, O Lord, You know it all. You have enclosed me behind and before, and [You have] placed Your hand upon me. Such [infinite] knowledge is too wonderful for me; it is too high [above me], I cannot reach it. Where can I go from Your Spirit? Or where can I flee from Your presence? If I ascend to heaven, You are there; if I make my bed in Sheol (the nether world, the place of the dead), behold, You are there. If I take the wings of the dawn, if I dwell in the remotest part of the sea, even there Your hand will lead me, and Your right hand will take hold of me. If I say, "Surely the darkness will cover me, and the night will be the only light around me," even the darkness is not dark to You and conceals nothing from You, but the night shines as bright as the day; darkness and light are alike to You. For You formed my innermost parts; You knit me [together] in my mother's womb. I will give thanks and praise to You, for I am fearfully and wonderfully made; wonderful are Your works, and my soul knows it very well. My frame was not hidden from You, when I was being formed in secret, and intricately and skilfully formed [as if embroidered with many colors] in the depths of the earth. Your eyes have seen my unformed substance; and in Your book were all written the days that were appointed for me, when as yet there was not one of them [even taking shape]. How precious also are Your thoughts to me, O God! How vast is the sum of them! If I could count them, they would outnumber the sand. When I awake, I am still with You. O that You would kill the wicked, O God; go away from me, therefore, men of bloodshed. For they speak against You wickedly, Your enemies take Your name in vain. Do I not hate those who hate You, O Lord? And do I not loathe those who rise up against You? I hate them with perfect and utmost hatred; they have become my enemies. Search me [thoroughly], O God, and know my heart; test me and know my anxious thoughts; and see if there is any wicked or hurtful way in me, and lead me in the everlasting way (Psalm 139:1-24 AMP).

This is my favorite psalm. The depth of it is amazing. David knew his God; he knew the love of the Father, the unconditional love of the Father, the love He had for him and all mankind. I have read this chapter over and over, and it always touches me. Take the time to read it slowly so you can really digest it and understand what it is saying to you and about you. You have to feel the love in this psalm. It is amazing. David ends by submitting his heart to the Lord, asking Him to search him, to know him completely, and then lead him in his life.

Intimacy is the only way to the Lord's heart. Think about it this way: If you have a relationship—any kind at all—you must cultivate it for it to grow. This is true for a husband and wife, a boyfriend and girlfriend, a parent and child, or friend to friend. If you don't work on a relationship, it will never be more than an association. It will never be more than superficial. If a husband and wife lived in the same house and talked with each other ten minutes a day, what kind of relationship would they have? They would only be acquaintances. They would not really be friends, not true lovers, and definitely not intimate, because intimacy only comes out of relationship and love.

> **Relationship:** The way in which two or more people or things are connected, or the state of being connected. (Synonyms: connection, relation, association, interconnection, correspondence.)[7]

> **Intimacy:** Close familiarity or friendship. (Synonyms: Closeness, affinity, attachment, friendship, familiarity.)[8]

A relationship between a husband and wife has to be built on intimacy, knowing one another on a deep level. This comes from communing with each other: conversation, communication, trust; it has to be a two way relationship. Both need to give one hundred percent to learn about each other, to give to one another their time, heart, and soul. If you do that, then you have a relationship, but this takes hours a day, weeks, months, and even years.

This is what David had with God, so much so that he spent hours before the Lord, worshiping and praising Him. David wasn't perfect. He was, by all accounts, an adulterer and a murderer; and yet, it is written that David was the apple of God's eye. Why? Because he was good? No, it was because after David recognized his errors, he was quick to repent and not repeat them. His heart was always for God. When you read about His relationship with the Father, it is truly inspirational. This guy loved the Lord with his whole heart, mind, and soul.

> And he answering said, Thou shalt love the Lord thy God with all thy heart, and with all thy soul, and with all

7. "Relationship | Definition of Relationship in English by Oxford Dictionaries," Oxford Dictionaries | English, accessed March 08, 2019, https://en.oxforddictionaries.com/definition/relationship.

8. "Intimacy | Definition of Intimacy in English by Oxford Dictionaries," Oxford Dictionaries | English, accessed March 08, 2019, https://en.oxforddictionaries.com/definition/intimacy.

thy strength, and with all thy mind; and thy neighbour as thyself (Luke 10:27 KJV).

Jesus is pretty clear here. This is a command. We are to love the Lord our God with all our heart, and with all our soul, with all our strength, and with all our mind. How do we do this? A relationship with a wife, husband, kids, friends, or whoever is hard enough; how can we have an intimate relationship with God? The Word says we have to seek Him while He may be found:

> Seek the Lord while He may be found, call upon Him while He is near. Let the wicked forsake his way, and the unrighteous man his thoughts; let him return to the Lord, and He will have mercy on him; and to our God, for He will abundantly pardon. "For My thoughts are not your thoughts, nor are your ways My ways," says the Lord. "For as the heavens are higher than the earth, so are My ways higher than your ways, and My thoughts than your thoughts" (Isaiah 55:6-9).

The Lord is not a harsh taskmaster and He's not an angry God. He is not a tyrant or a bully; He is not pushy or demanding. He is a loving, caring, compassionate, empathetic God and Father who wants a loving relationship with His children, allowing us to make that free will choice. He will not force us into anything—His love is that great. His love is so immense and incomprehensible that it is incredible that He would choose to commune with us, but still never cross our free will. As humans, our love can be demanding, one-sided, greedy, selfish, and conditional. Abba's love is unconditional. He wants to commune and fellowship with us, just as we are, knowing we are damaged. His love is so incredible and unselfish that He died for us:

> For God so loved the world that He gave His only begotten Son, that whoever believes in Him should not perish but have everlasting life. For God did not send

His Son into the world to condemn the world, but that the world through Him might be saved (John 3:16-17).

This love is so pure and so holy that it just blows me away. What a God! When I was first saved, I would look at some of the people in church and think, *Wow, all these people talk about is Jesus-this and Jesus-that, God-this and God-that, church-this and church-that. Surely life is more than this!* The problem was that I didn't know God intimately at that point. I was just learning, just beginning to seek, just pressing in. A survey by the American Bible Society was taken in 2013 and it indicated that 57% of Christians only read their Bibles four times *a year or less.*[9] An Ellis Research Survey for facts and trends found that only 16% of pastors were very satisfied with their personal prayer lives.[10]

We all want things from God, whether for ourselves or others: a better job, more money, a better marriage, a house, a car, love, peace, joy, a ministry, destiny. We always want the *presents* of God, but seldom pursue the *presence of God.* Pursuing that *requires* something from us: *time.* We have time for work, time for sports, time for family, time for TV, time for the Internet, time for playing games, time for drinks, drugs and porn, but we just don't have time for the Time-giver, God.

Come now, you who say, "Today or tomorrow we will go to such and such a city, spend a year there, buy and sell, and make a profit"; whereas you do not know what will happen tomorrow. For what is your life? It is even a vapor that appears for a little time and then vanishes away. Instead you ought to say, "If the Lord wills, we shall live and do this or that." But now you boast in your

9. Caleb K. Bell, "Poll: Americans Love the Bible but Don't Read It Much," Religion News Service, March 25, 2014, accessed March 08, 2019, https://religionnews.com/2013/04/04/poll-americans-love-the-bible-but-dont-read-it-much/

10. Toni Ridgaway, "[Prayer Statistics] Statistics on Prayer in the U.S.," ChurchLeaders, January 07, 2019, accessed March 08, 2019, https://churchleaders.com/pastors/pastor-articles/150915-u-s-statistics-on-prayer.html.

arrogance. All such boasting is evil. Therefore, to him who knows to do good and does not do it, to him it is sin (James 4:13-17).

We get so busy with the things of life, that we develop have a habit of putting God on a shelf, saying, "We'll get back to You later today, Lord." Yet later never comes (you know what I am talking about). We've all done this. The truth is that not one of us has a good excuse as to why we don't have time for the Lord. Time is universal, and we all have the same exact amount of time each week—everyone. We all have 168 hours per week. If we take 56 hours out for sleeping, and forty for work or school, that leaves us seventy-two hours a week for family and the rest. How many hours a week do we sit in front of the TV?

I'm not trying to make anyone feel bad or convicted. That's not my job. I am just laying out the facts. *We choose how we spend those seventy-two hours, but it is inevitable that they will be spent.* We should be seriously considering what we are investing in and how we use the precious time we have. We should be guarding what we see too. David wrote in Psalm 101:3 that he would not put anything base before his eyes, meaning he would not entertain himself with things that were beneath him. Once time has passed, it cannot be redeemed. As we hear from God, He will direct us into using our lives for the best options out there, the things that will bring us true personal satisfaction and build His kingdom too. Hearing from God requires something from us first, though.

Intimacy involves setting aside time for Him, just as we focus on someone other than ourselves when we fall in love. I can only share a man's perspective on this: You meet this beautiful woman, and she takes your breath away. Man, you just gotta see her again! You just can't get her out of your mind. She consumes your every waking moment. You get up in the morning and she is your first thought. You go to work (or school) and she's all you can think about. Work is almost done, and you are daydreaming about seeing her. Your buddies call, and say, "Hey man, let's go watch the football game" and almost, for a split second, you are tempted, but then she comes rushing back into your mind and the game flies out. All you want to do is see this beautiful woman again. You spend hours just talking to her. Everything she says is captivating. The more she speaks, the more you desire to be with her. Your feelings for her are growing to the point where you hate being away from her. Your relationship together has become intimate to the point that you finish her sentences or she finishes yours. A bond has formed like you never thought was possible. You know her, you know her likes and dislikes, what makes her happy and what makes her sad. It is almost like you can read her mind at times and she, yours. Crazy love has blossomed, and your hearts become one. You get married and become one flesh.

> For this reason a man shall leave his father and his mother and shall be joined [and be faithfully devoted] to his wife, and the two shall become one flesh. This mystery [of two becoming one] is great; but I am speaking with reference to [the relationship of] Christ and the church (Ephesians 5:31-32 AMP).

This is us! We are the body of Christ, and this is the relationship the Lord wants with us: one in which He is our every thought, and we are consumed with Him. Our love for Him overwhelms us; our desire to be with Him is greater than any other desire. Our Father desires this kind of relationship, and Jesus died so we could have it. He doesn't mind the hobbies and the sports. He made you exactly who you are. He just wants a relationship with you too, and He wants to be first in your life, greater in your heart than everything else. If He has your heart first, nothing else can have it. The Lord won't play second fiddle to anyone or anything. Me? I love Harleys, boats, and fast cars; I always have and always will, but I love the Lord more. As much as I loved cruising on my Hog (I've had three) or out fishing, I love my time with the Lord more. Usually when I was cruising down the road, whether with Pastor Graham or by myself, I would be mediating on the Word or on Abba. Pastor Graham did the same thing on his Ultra. *God wants to do everything with us.*

Years ago after my divorce, I prayed and I prayed earnestly for a woman who would love God more than she loves me (along with a list of other requirements and desires). I prayed and said, "Lord, this woman must be sold out to You. You must be her first love because if You are, then Your perfect love will flow out of her to me and others, and that love will be pure and undefiled. Lord, pure love does not have an agenda or a motive. It is not self-seeking nor does it have an entitlement attitude; it's powerful and unconditional like Your love, Lord."

Our heavenly Father wants this relationship with everyone; it's not just for some. Daddy's heart is for everyone to have this close, personal, and loving relationship with Him. If we would all pursue His presence, then the presents would come because He is a rewarder of those who diligently seek Him.

This is true! Everyone and anyone who desires a real relationship with the Lord can have one. How deep that relationship is depends on us. *We can have as much of God as we want.* This works in the natural the same way. A marriage can be as good or bad as we choose, and such is our life with the Holy Spirit. I was once talking with a woman, discussing her relationship with her husband. I told her that marriage in itself is hard if you have two people putting in one hundred percent, with all the worries and cares of the family, work, and the world. But a marriage where each partner is only putting in eighty percent is on a downward slope, and sliding fast. By the time you are at fifty percent, unless God intervenes, it is pretty much doomed. I told her this: "If you are honest, what percentage could you say you put into your relationship with your husband?" Her answer was sad: "Ten, maybe twenty percent!" Her marriage came to an end, and, unfortunately, her commitment level in her relationship with the Lord was even less.

Abba wants a hundred percent relationship with us. He wants a hundred percent of our heart, He doesn't want ninety, eighty, sixty, or ten. He wants us to worship Him with our whole heart from the core of our being. If we were to really grasp the fullness of what the Lord wants to do for us and through us, we would just drop everything and say, "Oh, yes, Lord, choose me, send me, use me! I surrender all to You, Lord. I will not stop pursuing You for anything the world has to offer because You are the most wonderful possibility there is for my life. I don't know what You have planned, but I know it is great and it will make me happy." And that is true: He promises us an extraordinary life in Him, an abundant life in Him, full of adventures in Him! (It's actually a *super-abundant* life!) Read it for yourself in John 10:10 sometime, but Paul in Ephesians 3:20 explains it in another way. What a promise! I love the Word of God. It is captivating beyond the wildest imagination.

> Now to Him who is able to [carry out His purpose and] do superabundantly more than all that we dare ask or think [infinitely beyond our greatest prayers, hopes, or dreams], according to His power that is at work within us (Ephesians 3:20 AMP).

Does this sound like a boring God to you? Does this sound like a Father that is sitting in heaven, saying, "My Son is coming back soon, so put your seat belt on, relax, take a little nap, and We will be there soon to pick you up. Oh, and while you are waiting, just do nothing"? No, absolutely not! Come on! His Word tells us that He is "*able* to [carry out His purpose and] *do superabundantly more* than all that we *dare ask or think* [infinitely beyond our greatest prayers, hopes, or dreams]." I don't know about you, but I can dare ask and dream quite a lot! So to those who have said, "I am a dreamer," take it up with God. He said He can *do superabundantly more than all* we can even imagine! But it doesn't stop there! It goes on to say "infinitely beyond our greatest prayers, hopes, or dreams" too! What prayers, hopes, and dreams do you have? I believe God's Word is true, so if He says it, I believe. Most of the dreams I have had have come from the Lord, and were confirmed by prophecy (some by complete strangers). How amazing!

Some have had people tell them they are dreamers, unrealistic, perhaps even foolish. Joseph was a dreamer, and look where it got him: He became prime minister of all Egypt! He did not take the most direct route, but in the end, he ended up exactly where the Lord wanted him to be. Joseph fulfilled his journey and walked out his book, and it was exhilarating, and pretty intense—and definitely not boring. Joseph did not wait for the Lord to come and get him; he took on every challenge and persevered; he pressed in and pressed on to the glory of the Lord. Stick with the dreams God has given you, just like Joseph did.

The Bible says we grow from glory to glory. It is a never-ending life because there is always more in Abba. There is always another level. The more you want, the more Jesus gives. The Holy Spirit is always looking for someone to pick up the ball and run with it. All we have to do is ask.

> Ask, and it will be given to you; seek, and you will find; knock, and it will be opened to you. For everyone who asks receives, and he who seeks finds, and to him who knocks it will be opened (Matthew 7:7-8).

Have you ever noticed that the Word of God seems somewhat conditional? We have to do our part, then—and only then—does the Lord do His: *Ask,* and it will be given to you; *seek,* and you will find; *knock,* and it will be opened to you. For *everyone who asks* receives, and he who *seeks* finds, and to him who *knocks* it will be opened. If this is the case, then what happens when we *call* on the Lord? I mean, really *call* on the Lord from the very depth of our hearts because we want the Creator of the Universe to turn our world upside down? We want to walk *an extreme walk with Jesus* and we have decided we will not walk another day settling for second best. We have made the decision that we want to sell out to the Lord one hundred percent! We are all-in with no compromise: It's all or nothing.

> I know your works, that you are neither cold nor hot. I could wish you were cold or hot. So then, because you are lukewarm, and neither cold nor hot, I will vomit you out of My mouth (Revelation 3:15-16).

There is no gray area in Christ. Jesus said so, and whether we believe it or not, He said it. I feel sorry for the lukewarm believer (or church), the one who allowed the fire of the Holy Spirit to burn out and allowed sin to creep in, the church (or person) who doesn't preach the complete written Word and preaches a watered-down version instead.

We are all-in now, knowing *anything we ask, we will receive*. When we seek, we will find; and when we knock, it will be opened. May Jesus stir up the gifts that are in you and activate the call upon your life through the Holy Spirit. The Lord does the rest when we call on Him. I call on Him out of desperation, knowing there is more, and all I want is more of Him. When I started calling on Him, things started happening.

> Call to Me and I will answer you, and tell you [and even show you] great and mighty things, [things which have been confined and hidden], which you do not know and understand and cannot distinguish (Jeremiah 33:3).

When I started calling on the Lord, nations started opening up to me. I found myself in different countries, speaking, with incredible miracles occurring just like it says will happen in the Word of God! Hmm, just what Jesus said would happen in Mark 16:15-18!

Before I close this chapter, I want to share an example of intimacy. My last two trips to Indonesia were completely different. Before leaving for the first one, the Holy Spirit had another guy and I spend five hours a day in the Spirit (praying in tongues, no English). We did this for 100 days (or 500 hours). There were some just outstanding things that happened on this trip. (I shared some of them earlier.) And I mean, truly amazing things. I went back a year and a half later, and ministered there again. The trip was a success in the way of great impartation, speaking into leaders and pastors' lives, words of knowledge, and prophecy, but not the same as before. I felt that something was missing. They brought an orphan who was severely handicapped, and I prayed and nothing happened. I went back to my hotel room that night filled with disappointment. I cried out to the Lord and asked why nothing had happened. I told Him, "This would have glorified Your name, let alone healed that child." I heard nothing. When I returned to Australia, I was driving down the road and the Holy Spirit spoke to me and asked me, "John, what was the difference between the first trip and the second one?" I answered that in the first trip so much more happened, and the second trip seemed only about equipping and impartation.

Isn't it awesome that when you miss it, the Holy Spirit just tells you how it is? He said, "No, that was not the difference. Before the first trip, you spent five hours a day for 100 days with Me in preparation (intimacy). Before the second trip, you were all caught up in family issues and other things, and did not spend the time with Me." Wow, reality check! I repented of letting things come before my relationship with the Lord. Before my last trip to America, I was asked by the Holy Spirit to spend five hours a day with Him again, so I did. That trip was incredible. When God is in it, it is not a burden.

I share this with you, so as you can see that the deeper we go with Abba in true intimacy, the greater level of glory we can walk in. If I have learned anything in my walk, it is this: *Intimacy is the key that opens doors and unlocks everything.*

King David had an extremely intimate walk with Abba. He was the apple of God's eye—again, not because he was perfect (far from it, really), but because his heart was all about the Father. We should take the time to study David more. Jesus came to bring us back into relationship with the Father. I urge you to press into the Lord in a deeper way. Again, it does not matter where you are in your walk. There is more, much more for all of us. The purpose of this chapter is to bring everyone to a place of desiring more of God:

> Deep calls unto deep at the noise of Your waterfalls; all
> Your waves and billows have gone over me (Psalm 42:7).

Deeper, wider, higher! The Holy Spirit wants to soar with you like an eagle. Don't hold back! There is a deep walk with Jesus for everyone. Just let go and let God! We can say, "Daddy, have Your way in my life. I release it all to You, and I trust You, Lord, (Psalms 3:5-6)." Then we have started a stronger, deeper walk. Hold on! It will be amazing, to say the least. You will say and do things which you would have deemed impossible before; but with the Lord, all things are possible.

My heart is that all will have an intimate relationship with the Lord, so intimate that it will be evident to all who know you. And that it will not just be lip service but a real heart connection with Abba. May the love of the Father so consume you that it will overflow in and through you, and spill out onto others. May you be full of pure, undefiled love, the love of the Father! Amen.

What if we could be truly honest with ourselves? *What if we asked God this:* Where am I truly at with You, Lord? *What if* we asked the Lord to bring us into a deeper walk with Him? *What if* after reading this, you prayed and told God that you knew there was more and you wanted it? *What if* you said, "Abba, I want all of You; I want a more intimate relationship with You. I want everything You have for me, no matter what it looks like"? *What if* you got to this place and said, "Daddy, I surrender all to You right now! Use me for Your glory. I want a deeper life in You, and I do not want to settle for anything less anymore. I am not sure what that even looks like, but I want more of You, much more. Please meet me, Lord"?

Having an intimate relationship is life-changing. Everything flows from intimacy with Jesus: signs, wonders, creative miracles, the release of our destiny in Him, even our ability to walk in Him. Being filled to overflowing with the Holy Spirit is intimacy, and nothing is more intense than that. The Holy Spirit is waiting to take you further, deeper, and wider than you have ever been before. Just *ask Him, seek Him, and keep knocking.* He is willing; He actually yearns for it. Are you willing? I encourage everyone to go deeper. The deeper I go, the more I see my need to go deeper still! Hanging with Jesus is the coolest thing I have ever done. I would not give this relationship up for anything or anyone. The Savior of the World wants to hang out with me, and more importantly, *you!* Surrendering everything and trusting Him with your entire life is *extreme to the max.* Are you in?

Chapter Nine: How Close?

How *close, Lord? What if* we were to enter into a place of reckless abandonment in God? *What if* we were to just let go of everything we knew or had done—up until now? *What if* we surrendered all afresh, and let go and let God? *What if* we were to come to Abba with no expectations, no list, no asking? *What if* we just came to Him with thanksgiving, praise, and worship—and nothing else? Pressing into Him for Him, to go to the next level of intimacy. Worshiping our Creator for who He is, and not for what He can do for us. I was once going through a real wilderness period and was calling out to the Lord. I was asking Him where He was, and reminding Him of His Word, which says He would never leave us or forsake us. Yet I felt so abandoned, so left on my own; it was painful. I went to sleep, waking up to hearing the word "ingratitude." I thought, *Really? What do I have to be grateful for?*

At that time in the natural, I felt like I had just wasted three-and-a-half years of my life and that I had been held back from moving forward in the things of God. What seemed to be a God-thing ended up being everything, but I was angry. The Devil had robbed these years of my life through this situation.

> **Ungrateful:** Not feeling or showing gratitude. (Synonyms: unappreciative, unthankful, thankless, ungracious.) [11]

11. "Ungrateful | Definition of Ungrateful in English by Oxford Dictionaries," Oxford Dictionaries | English, accessed March 08, 2019, https://en.oxforddictionaries.com/definition/ungrateful.

As I pondered this ingratitude idea, He spoke to me again, saying, "What about the very breath you take, and every day I have given you?" You have already read enough about my life to see why I should have been appreciating that. I didn't think I would make it to thirty, so when I hit forty, I thought, *This is huge!* When fifty came I was blown away.

When you consider the many times you should have been dead, but nope, here you are: alive for His glory, you suddenly become grateful. Then you start praying things like: "Lord, if You tarry, may I have 120 years and be preaching the gospel until the end?"

> And the Lord said, "My Spirit shall not strive with man forever, for he is indeed flesh; yet his days shall be one hundred and twenty years" (Genesis 6:3).

When the Lord Himself shows up and starts showing you all the times He rescued you, right next to all the times everyone else abandoned you (and I mean everyone—even the ones who said they never would), suddenly you are grateful. When you realize He was the only One *still standing* with you, gratitude starts pouring into your heart. When you realize that only God the Father, the Son, and the Holy Spirit have your back, a reverent fear overwhelms you.

> The [reverent] fear of the Lord [that is, worshiping Him and regarding Him as truly awesome] is the beginning and the preeminent part of wisdom [its starting point and its essence], and the knowledge of the Holy One is understanding and spiritual insight. For by me (wisdom from God) your days will be multiplied, and years of life shall be increased (Proverbs 9:10-11 AMP).

So when we come to that place of reverent fear, that place of awe, that place of knowing our life is not ours but His, we suddenly gain a new perspective and come to a place of total reckless abandonment. This is the place where we cry out, "Lord, not my will but Your will be done. May it be done on earth as it is in heaven for all my life. Lord, use me for Your glory, I surrender all to You now. Daddy, use me; my heart is Yours! Give me Your heart, Abba." We come to a place where we finally say, "Enough is enough. I will no longer try to make it happen! I give it all to You, Jesus. I place my life, my will, and my destiny at the foot of the cross. I truly surrender all to You that my life will be Yours. It is no longer my life that lives, but Yours that lives through me, that I may glorify Your name in everything I do."

I am at a place now in which all I want is more of Him. Deeper, wider, higher—all that He is: That's all that I want. I want to be so close to Him that when He speaks, everything in my heart responds with yes and amen. May I have no hesitation, no questioning. May I be so recklessly abandoned that His will is my will.

> My sheep hear My voice, and I know them, and they follow Me (John 10:27).

I want to be so close that when that still, quiet voice speaks, I am able to say, "Yes, Lord." In this loud crazy world we live in, we have to stay close to the Spirit of the Living God so that when He speaks, we recognize His voice instantly. The world is screaming for our attention 24/7; the Devil, that dirtbag, is trying to get us to miss the mark all the time. With the times more chaotic than ever and the Devil's time is running out, his mission is to get us so busy that we miss what the Spirit is trying to get us to do.

> The thief does not come except to steal, and to kill, and to destroy. I have come that they may have life, and that they may have it more abundantly (John 10:10).

In this verse, Jesus is telling us that the only purpose the thief (the Devil) has is to steal, and what does he have to steal? It is the Word. If he can steal the Word, you have no power. He can kill us in one of two ways: He can take you out (literally kill you) or kill your dreams. Either one will prevent you from going forward. The third thing he does is destroy. At all costs, the Devil will try to destroy your destiny. He tried it with Joseph: He thought throwing him in prison would bury him alive. He tried it with Moses as a baby, and then he tried it with

Jesus. The Devil does not have anything new, but do not underestimate him. He is a legalist par excellence. If he gets in somehow, it is usually because we have opened the door for him and allowed him to enter—legally. That is actually the only way he can get in after you have had generational curses broken off of you and repented of your past and you are born again.

Jesus went on to share the good news in this passage. He says that He came that they may have life, and that they may have it more abundantly. In the Amplified Bible it says, "I came that they may have and enjoy life, and have it in abundance *[to the full, till it overflows]."* How does this work? Well, to have life like this only occurs when we are *totally submerged in Him.* When He becomes the center of our life, when we can say it is no longer I that live, but Christ that lives in me:

> I have been crucified with Christ; it is no longer I who live, but Christ lives in me; and the life I now live in the flesh I live by faith in the Son of God, who loved me and gave Himself for me (Galatians 2:20).

When we desire more of Him than we desire the things of the world, then and only then can we reach the pinnacle of what we are truly called to be in Him. In the chapter on witty ideas, I shared an example of this. The Word says:

> For what man knows the things of a man except the spirit of the man which is in him? (1 Corinthians 2:11).

My idea came through a dream, and then the Lord told me what I was to do with it. Later I listened to man and not God and lost the gain from the idea. I was at home one day and received a call from a friend, who asked me if I was watching a show on TV about the news. When I said I wasn't, he told me to turn it on. I turned on the TV and there was my invention in a slightly-improved form on a commercial, and even the commercial wasn't much different than mine. I went to the Lord, and I was angry. I asked Him, "Lord, how could You let this happen?" He answered, "I told you what to do, and you did not listen to Me. Instead you listened to man, and not Me." I didn't like that answer, so I thought I would rephrase the question. "But Lord, how could You let Your idea be stolen? It was for the kingdom!" Again He answered, "It was never for My kingdom; it was for yours." You could have knocked me over with a feather! I was shocked. I thought, *Wow, how could that be?* This was simply incomprehensible to my mind. I was undone, so I asked Him to help me understand. He said, "You would only have tipped Me for it." Again, I was shocked. I thought, *No, Lord, that can't be right.* Think about the reality of the word *tipped.* God owns everything, and here He was saying that I would have only tossed Him whatever I thought I *had* to give Him. Crazy! And this was after it had been prophesied that I would give ninety percent of my income into the kingdom and use the ten percent I had left for my family and that I would never be able to spend that ten percent in my lifetime. How could this be true of me? The Lord was saying, *John, wake up to yourself! I know the condition of your heart: Things have it, not Me.* I was devastated. *Could this be true?* Only God knows the true condition of our hearts. We may think we understand ourselves, but only He really knows. We can say all the right things and do the right things on the outside, but only the Lord knows the inside.

So how does one get past this? How does one deal with God saying that things have your heart? How was I to change that? Good questions. The Lord has had me give up everything a few times in my life. He has reduced me to two suitcases and a few boxes. Is having literally nothing for everyone? I would say definitely not, but for me, those times have been the seasons of my greatest growth. One day I phoned a friend and told them I could now understand what Paul meant when he said:

> Not that I speak in regard to need, for I have learned in whatever state I am, to be content: I know how to be abased, and I know how to abound. Everywhere and in all things I have learned both to be full and to be hungry, both to abound and to suffer need. I can do all things through Christ who strengthens me (Philippians 4:11-13).

In whatever state you are in, whether you have things or you don't, you are content. You are not moved because you have Christ. He is more than enough because in Him, you have everything, and without Him, you have nothing. Having gone through all these things has brought me to a place where I can say "Your will be done on earth as it is in heaven." How close? How close do you want to get to the Lord? What are you willing to give up for Him? There is a cost, and it may cost you everything.

Angie and I were watching a Christian documentary the other day. It was unbelievable, yet shouldn't have been. We, in the Western world, have it very easy. Don't get me wrong. I know there are some who have it hard, very hard, but next to this documentary, wow! They were interviewing a man from India. As a Christian, he had seen many Christians martyred for their beliefs, and he had been beaten, stabbed (they showed his scars), and left for dead. He did not die, but recovered and is still preaching the gospel; but in the end, he believes he will die for it. Now that is commitment: all-in, sold-out, paying the ultimate price, walking an extreme walk with Jesus—to the death if required. How close would you have to be with the Lord to drink that cup?

On the whole, Christians in the Western world have become like McDonald's: They want instant everything. We have a drive-through mentality, a quick-fix attitude and want everything done in one day—or it is too hard. However, Jesus said,

> Go therefore and make disciples of all the nations (Matthew 28:19).

What is a disciple?

> **Disciple:** A personal follower of Christ during his life, especially one of the twelve Apostles. (Synonyms: apostle, follower.)

People want everything given to them free of charge. There is a spirit of entitlement upon the entire Western world. Being a disciple of Jesus is an ongoing journey; there are no quick fixes. A price is required.

Oddly enough, we accept that idea in many areas of life, but not the things of God. If our child says he or she wants to be a doctor, we say, "That is wonderful. We will support you in that endeavor." Then we tell them that if they want to become a doctor, they will need good marks in high school, and will be required to go to a college or university, where they will also need excellent grades. When they are done there, they will be able to begin as a doctor. We also explain that this is going to take seven years more school after high school, and longer if they want to be a specialist in a particular field. Once they finish all that, they will continue to take refresher courses from time to time, to stay current and on top of their game. Once they pay the price, they will have a rewarding career and it will be good, but the next ten years of their life are going to require a lot of study and development. (There is a price that has to be paid.)

Nobody I know who is anyone in the Lord just got there without the same kind of preparation and hard work. I love reading testimonies of some of the generals of old or even the current ones. They have all paid a price to get where they are today. Apostles, prophets, evangelists, pastors, and teachers are all still disciples studying the Word and seeking the face of God. They are learning and paying a price. If you have not read the testimonies of some of these mighty men and women of the faith, I encourage you to do so. They will blow you away. When others were doing this and that, these leaders were pressing in. They were walking by faith and not by sight.

When everyone said they were crazy, that their vision couldn't be done, that it was not God, these people faithfully obeyed and went ahead anyway. (Some of those naysayers came on board after all the hard work was done, and the price was paid.) The testimonies of those obedient visionaries are amazing. Each one had to deny themselves and take up their cross. In fact, many of them worked in the face of strong opposition. A price was paid. If I've learned anything in the kingdom, it is that nothing comes without a cost, except salvation. And that actually came with a very high price, but it was not one we had to pay. Jesus paid the ultimate price, a ransom, and for us. Our life begins with our salvation, and after that, we are led to submit and pay a price just as Jesus did. And as we do that, we also reap a harvest like Him.

So what am I saying? Even if all you want is a closer relationship with the Lord, even if you just want to praise Him, worship Him, and honor Him for who He truly is, even that requires a price. That price is your time, as I mentioned in the last chapter on intimacy. The Lord wants us to seek Him with everything we have. It is up to us how much time we give Him, so *"how close" becomes up to us*. He wants all of us. He wants our hearts, He wants our praise, our adoration, our selfless worship. He wants us to take time out of our busy lives to say, "Daddy, I love You, and thank You for being You. Thank You for being my God. Thank You, Lord, for the way You have intervened in my life. I just want to thank You." Doing this would help us conquer our troubles, and then usher us into a brand new life filled with peace:

> Be anxious for nothing, but in everything by prayer and supplication, with thanksgiving, let your requests be made known to God; and the peace of God, which surpasses all understanding, will guard your hearts and minds through Christ Jesus (Philippians 4:6-7).

If you are anxious, only the Holy Spirit can bring peace, and that starts with thanksgiving, praise, and worship. We serve an awesome God who only wants to love us and spend time with us, so we can, in turn, love others in the same way. Again, this only comes out of relationship; it is never God who has the problem. He is ever waiting on us to surrender everything to Him so He can take over. We have the One and only true Living God: God the Father, God the Son, and God the Holy Spirit, all in One, and One in all, the real God. He is alive! We have a God who listens to us, speaks to us, answers our prayers, and does miracles on our behalf—and yet we will only give Him a portion of us, instead of everything. This is a wonder in itself, don't you think? This state of affairs has been going on since man fell in the garden! How can we be so deceived and dense? We show a reluctance to surrender and give all we are to the Creator of the world. It's crazy, but true.

Daddy only wants us to come to the end of ourselves. Here's a good way to begin:

> *Father, I surrender all and I mean it. I've said it a hundred times, only to have the Holy Spirit bring some new thing to the surface which I have not surrendered. Lord, I trust You to purify my heart before You. I don't want anything in me that is not of You. I only want Your Spirit and my spirit: If there's anything else, show it to me and I will renounce it, and command it to go in Jesus' name.*

> *Holy Spirit, search my heart, try my anxieties and if there is anything displeasing to You, remove it. It has to go. Holy Spirit, I give You permission to search the depths of my heart and soul to find anything that would hold me back from Your fullness. Lord, I want to be used by You for Your glory. I ask, Lord, that You would shine Your rays of glory into my heart, mind, and soul. Heal all the wounds and scars I have, whether through my own doing or through another's. Lord, I forgive everyone who has hurt, used, or abused me over the course of my life. Through my forgiveness, I know that I am forgiven of any pain or hurt I have caused others. I ask the blood to wash over me now. I am forgiven, healed, and delivered in the name of Jesus.*

Once when I was preaching, I was going down the line praying for people as the Spirit led me. I came to this guy who asked if I would ask the Lord to give him my anointing. Before I could say anything, a lady who was ministering with me said to him, "Are you prepared to pay the price he has paid to be here?" She knew some of my testimony and some of the walk I had to endure just to get to that point. Then I looked at the young man and said, "This is not *my* anointing, so I cannot give it away. Only the Lord can give or take an anointing."

For the gifts and the calling of God are irrevocable (Romans 11:29).

By disobedience, sin, or not submitting to the Holy Spirit, one can grieve the Holy Spirit and He will withdraw, and the power one had can drop, but the gift or call is never taken. What a good God we have! What an exceptional, outstanding, brilliant God and Father! We are incredibly blessed to have Him. We should all desire Him in a greater way. The world is perishing. We need to get past ourselves and press into Abba. We need to find out what and where we fit in and get it done. Time is short! Jesus is coming back, and He is coming back *soon*. Let Him not find us sleeping or so caught up in the things of the world that we miss Him. That would be tragic. Now is the time to seek Him. His Word says to seek Him while He may be found:

> Seek the Lord while He may be found, call upon Him while He is near (Isaiah 55:6).

And again:

> Then you will call upon Me and go and pray to Me, and I will listen to you. And you will seek Me and find Me, when you search for Me with all your heart. I will be found by you, says the Lord, and I will bring you back from your captivity (Jeremiah 29:12-14).

The Lord wants a relationship with you—not an acquaintance, not an association, and not a: *Hey, how's it going*? The Lord wants a full-blown, through-and-through, complete-package relationship with you. Yes, a love affair, a romance; we are the body of Christ. He is coming back for His bride. Okay, that might sound weird and maybe I have lost some of the guys, but this is getting deep. If I wasn't the one writing this, I would be thinking, *Slow down there, big fella*. But I can't write something else because this is the truth. I have come to a place of loving the Lord so much and so deeply that I only want to fulfill everything written in my book (not this one, but the one He wrote about me), and more importantly, I want a deeper and more intimate relationship with my Creator, my Father, my Savior, and the Holy Spirit, who dwells inside me. I want to have a relationship with the One who has never left me, never forsaken me, never abandoned me, who has always been there through thick and thin, even if I didn't see Him or feel Him. The One who always has had my back and never screwed me over! Are you kidding me? How could I not want an intimate relationship with Abba? He is the omnipotent, omnipresent, omniscient, benevolent, unstoppable God who is still creating the universe!

So *how close* do we need to get? Again, that depends on us! The Holy Spirit will never take us where we do not want to go. He is a gentleman. He will quicken you, speak to you, ask you, and even tell you to do something, but He will never *make* you do it. He will not force you into anything. Unfortunately, many people see God as a harsh taskmaster, forcing us to do things they do not want to do. In most cases, religion puts these unbearable or undoable burdens on people, not God. This perception has made us think that if that is God or religion, I don't what it (or Him). Religion or religious people have left a bad taste in many people's mouths. This is not God. Even Jesus did not like religion or religious acts. Jesus was focused on the kingdom, not placing burdens and heavy yokes upon people. He was always rebuking the Pharisees and Sadducees for the unrealistic demands they put people under, and how they tried to put people under the law, forcing them to maintain traditions they couldn't even keep themselves. Jesus came to bring us back to the Father and bring us back into the fellowship that Adam once had. He came to bring freedom, fellowship, and relationship.

> Therefore if the Son makes you free, you shall be free indeed (John 8:36).

Jesus wants to have us sold out to Him, and that only comes through relationship. We need to press into Him. I have pressed into Him, and where I am today is amazing because of Him. I have a closer relationship with the Lord than I have ever had with any person. He never talks behind your back, betrays you, or judges, condemns, or criticizes. If you err, He has the Holy Spirit bring conviction to you, which in turn can bring correction, which He never forces on you because He honors your free will. And while He is doing all that, He is also encouraging you and helping you. The closer you get to the Lord, the more the things of the world and the things that held you back start falling off. You get to a place in which they all just drop away: all those bad habits, addictions, and besetting sins. The presence of the Lord becomes much more important than anything the world can offer. You become captivated by Him, and everything else dims in comparison. You desire the things of the Lord rather than the many pursuits that held your attention before. Does that mean you give up everything? Sports, hunting, fishing, cooking, shopping, crafting? Nope, it means they are no longer the priority in your life. He is instead. *You just do all those things with Him.* He wants to become so much of our world that He goes with us everywhere we go. He wants to do it all with you.

I will give you a quick example. I went out fishing with my friend Wayne and my son Chris. I have known Wayne for sixteen years or so. He is a crazy fisherman, been fishing all his life. Anyway we were fishing, and Wayne and Chris were pulling them in like crazy. Me? Nothing. Chris got this snapper: It was so big it was nearly pulling him overboard. He was very young at the time, he just wouldn't let go of the rod. I had to pull it in for him. As it got later in the night, Wayne and Chris both fell asleep, so there I was, sitting and waiting. I wanted to catch a fish so badly. About an hour later, I said to the Lord, "Father, I want to catch a fish." I heard him say so clearly, "You are a fisher of men." God has a sense of humor. He wants to be with you, and have fun with you. I answered, "Yeah, I get that, but one fish out of this ocean is all I am asking for." Then bam, my line was hit. I ended up with the biggest snapper of the trip! Both of them slept through the whole thing, but I finally reeled it in and got it into the cooler. Wayne woke and when I told him about it he thought I was putting one over him. When Chris woke, he thought I was telling a fish story too. Both of them did until Wayne looked inside the cooler. It was big! So does the Holy Spirit want you to give up everything? Nope (unless it is ungodly). *He wants to do it all with you.* I have had so much fun with the Holy Spirit. The things I have done with Him have been exhilarating.

Yes, I have given up some things, but I have taken up new things which I enjoy better. I like living on the edge, so of course the things I do with the Lord are on the edge too—sometimes even over it. I want an extreme walk with Jesus, and I will not settle for second best. Nothing and no one will hold me back from walking this intimate walk with the Lord. Jesus is the ultimate, extreme Walker: no one has ever walked His walk and lived and is now sitting at the right hand of Abba like Him! How cool is that? How cool is He? The soon and coming King!

I will say it again: Tell them I am coming! Tell them I am coming! Tell them I am coming! Do not take this lightly: Jesus is coming, and He is coming soon.

Jesus is the key to life, intimacy is the key to relationship, relationship is the key to miracles, and miracles are the key to the harvest. Press in for your keys! Now is the time, for the harvest is ripe. Abba is looking for the harvesters.

What if everyone reading this book said, "Lord, I want to be so close to You, so close that I could feel Your heartbeat, and I could know Your will for my life"? *What if* we all said, "Lord, transform my heart so my life and my desires would be pleasing to You, and so I would only pursue what You want me to pursue"? *What if* we all got so close (how close?) *so close* that we all fulfilled the purposes and destinies written in our books in heaven? *What if* we desired to walk in a deeper life of intimacy with the Lord? Oh, how that could change the world for His glory!

Chapter Ten: The Elephant in the Room

So I guess it is time to address the *elephant in the room*!

You may be thinking, *Whoa, John!* **How** *in the world could I ever spend three to five hours a day with the Lord?* **Why** *should I do that?* **Where** *do you do that?* **What** *would that look like?* **How** *did* **you** *get to that in your life to begin with?* If you are wondering these questions, you are in perfect company. I was once sharing about the awesome time Angie and I had with the Lord with a friend of mine. I was on a roll, describing how tangible Jesus' presence with us was, and how Angie had received a couple visions in this time. After a bit, he looked at me and asked, "What do you *do* for three or four hours?" Now this brother walks as an apostle; he is strong in the Lord, but he was a little baffled. At that moment, I realized that *this discipline is different in everyone's life*. At the same time, I realized that everyone could practice what Angie and I were doing to some measure, as led by the Lord.

All of us have the ability, like Peter on that rooftop so long ago, to seek the Lord, praying, worshipping, and praising the Lord. Peter had a vision that led to him understanding that God wanted to include the Gentiles in His plan in a way that Peter had not been open to before. God gave Peter a vision as Peter worshipped Him. God has not changed, so if He wants to do that today with you or somebody else, He will. Did Peter plan to have that vision? No! Was Peter seeking God for that purpose? Again, the answer is no. What happened to Peter was the result of his relationship with the Father, *a relationship that every born-again Christian shares.*

This time we spend with God is a natural response to God. Exactly how it is built in your life may not be the same as it is with Angie and me, but that is not important. This is the important part: *Every one of us needs time with God*, when we speak to Him and listen to Him, and when we praise Him and invest in Him. It is about relationship, and it is Abba's will that we all have a relationship with Him and everything comes out of that. Angie and I get up every morning eager to turn on the praise and worship music, then we make coffee and sit down with the Holy Spirit. We have been doing this for so long that it would seem odd if we didn't. Do we feel like doing it every day? In actual fact, 95-97% of the time the answer would be yes, but once in a while, my flesh rises up and I think, *Let's not. I don't feel like it.* The Word instructs us to crucify the flesh and walk in the Spirit, so I do it anyway. Even on those days when I have sat before the Lord and thought, *Lord, I ain't got nothing*, He still breaks through. When you simply bask in worship music, letting it wash over you, your heart is moved.

When I first began this, I did not spend three hours with the Lord, but it did not take long to get there. And it was not intentional that I ever did. I do not use a timer. We simply press into Abba, and that is the coolest thing I have ever done: praying, worshipping, praising, praying in the Spirit, and reading the Word. Suddenly an hour has gone by, then two, then three.

As I said before, this will not look the same in everyone's life. The Lord has told us to do what we do. It is related to fulfilling the call on our lives. The Lord may not ask you to spend that much time with Him all at once, if ever. Your time with Him will fit your calling and your life. Your time may be spent over the course of the day: before work, lunch breaks, in the car, before you go to sleep, at midday—whenever fits in your life. Rest assured about this: *He truly wants to spend time with you.* And He will show up and your walk with Him will deepen as a result.

Why is this important? Again, this is about relationship. The Word says God is a jealous God, not in a weird way, but in a protective and loving one. We are His creation, so He yearns for our attention, our adoration, our praise, our worship. He wants fellowship with each and every one of us. He wants you to come to Him, warts and all: He knows everything about you anyway, and He still wants to have a relationship with you. The closer I got with the Lord, the more the things of the world fell off, and the more I have been transformed and freed. Some things that seemed very important at one time meant little over time. Spending time with Jesus has changed me: He's changed my heart and my perspectives. He's made me happier as a result. This time has also been when He has chosen to share His heart with me and shown me my future path. As He does this, He will open the doors that need to be opened. The Word says we are to love the Lord with all our hearts, mind, strength and soul. Until we know who God truly is—personally, it is hard to love Him in that way. Spending time with Him is how we know Him, and vice versa. So, yeah, this is really important. *Let Him build it in your life.*

As I already mentioned, *when* you do this, it is a personal thing. Begin by seeking the Lord about what best fits your life. He will be faithful to show you. When I began, as I said earlier, the Lord woke me up, urging me to seek Him early in the day. Before that, I didn't wake early. For the next fifteen years, the Holy Spirit woke me every morning at five. I never had to set a clock—ever. For me, it has always been: morning, music, coffee, and Jesus. Why did He choose five in the morning? I am not a morning person and I had five boys, so I needed that time by myself with the Lord before everyone else got up. Once they were up, it could get just a bit loud to spend time with the Lord; but most importantly, my time with God prepared me for whatever my day threw at me: in my family, my workplace, and life in general. It was not (and is not) a religious thing I did. It happened out of my desperation to walk closer with the One who created me and called me by name, the One who pulled me from the snare of the Devil and saved me from hell, and the One who had placed me on this new and wonderful path. The Lord simply asked me to get up and seek Him early with a grateful heart, and I did. I have never regretted doing it. Just knowing Abba wants to spend time with Angie and me alone is worth getting up for! And five in the morning is what worked for me and it still does! Then I had five boys, and worked all hours in real estate. I didn't have a lot of time at night. By then, I was too tired, so this was my option and I took it cheerfully. Today all that has changed, but my habit remains. Seek the Lord about what this should look like in your life.

We spend our time with the Lord every morning in our home in our living room. For you, it can be anywhere you choose: It could be a prayer closet, it could be your workplace, a spot at your school, out on your boat, on your Hog, in a field. *The "where" is not as important as the time.* Abba wants your time just as any good father wants to spend time with his sons and daughters. *The only important aspect of where you meet with God has to do with your ability to be free to hear and express yourself there.* Many people have a "spot" and this is helpful. I know a friend who has a quiet place that is already set up for her. All she has to do is sit down, open up that Bible that stays in that spot, and immerse herself in God's Word, or close her eyes and pour out her heart. She can quietly listen, hear from God, and pick up the notebook she keeps there to journal what He speaks to her. Everything she needs is already there. Sometimes she walks and prays as she walks. Another person I know spends time in a forest behind her home. Another friend has a place in his basement where he can just be alone with God, and he goes there daily. Some of these people play music part of the time or all the time they are seeking God, and others do not. The point is this: You need to find that place where you can let go of all the thoughts, worries and cares that you carry, releasing them all to the Father. As you press into Him, He will show up, true to His Word:

> Call to Me and I will answer you, and tell you [and even show you] great and mighty things, [things which have been confined and hidden], which you do not know and understand and cannot distinguish (Jeremiah 33:3 AMP).

When you find your place—the one in which you and only you— can come boldly into the throne room of mercy and grace, then you can call upon the name of the Lord and He will answer. So your time with the Lord will not look like mine or someone else's. Yours will be uniquely your own, as directed by God.

This whole process is all about you and the Lord, your relationship with Him. He doesn't want anything else from you. Everything else comes out of relationship, and your desire to spend time with Him. Don't get freaked out about how much time you spend either: *It is about quality, not quantity.* Remember what Jesus said about the two dudes praying: one waffled and thought about how well he looked and how well he did and who was watching him, and other was humble and right to the point. Jesus preferred the one that was to the point and honest. This isn't about a show. The reason I share about the time we spend in the Lord is to encourage others to do the same, because power comes from prayer. The bulk of the time I pray is spent praying in the Spirit, so I don't even know what I am praying anyway. Only He does. The Word says that we should all be praying in the Spirit because it builds up our inner man when we pray in the holy language. If you do not pray in tongues, ask the Holy Spirit for this free gift and He will give it to you. The point here is that your time with God be focused and thoughtful, in which you are humbled before Him and He pours into you, so that you can rise and meet the day. And further, so you can be led in him to do everything He has called you to do in your life.

I truly hope this has helped. I have been asked about this by many people, and my heart is to encourage and bring everyone to a place of greater intimacy and relationship with our loving Father, so we will all exalt the name of Jesus, and hear from Him daily. I want everyone to come into the fullness of the call of God on their lives and have an intimate relationship with Jesus.

Intimacy only comes out of desire, followed by discipline and consistency, so it takes time and practice, but it does come in time. Everyone has days in which we struggle pressing in to the Lord. The world vies for our time and attention through appointments, work, and more. The enemy even tries to distract our thoughts when we pray, trying to get our minds to simply wander off. Seriously. Just consider this: Here we are, pressing in, trying to worship, praying and seeking Him, and we start thinking about lunch or any number of things. Fortunately, we have the Word to come back to as our focus. This is key to breaking through; we have literally prayed this thousands of times:

> Casting down arguments and every high thing that exalts itself against the knowledge of God, bringing every thought into captivity to the obedience of Christ (2 Corinthians 10:5).

Angie and I are not exempt from this. It happens to everyone. The Devil does not want any of us to come into the relationship that God prepared for us with Jesus. Let me give you an analogy: The Lord has told me to get in shape for what was coming (i.e. ministry, travel). So we put the treadmill right into the living room, so it is not out of sight or out of mind, but right in my face. It is amazing what comes up! Almost anything prevents me from getting on that thing. I have fifteen to eighteen kilograms to lose (thirty-five to forty pounds). I have done it before but allowed it to come back, and putting it on is a lot easier than taking it off. I do get on that treadmill, but not to the extent that it takes to lose that weight. Everything and anything can come between me and my goal. What is required? Discipline! I must stop making excuses, and press in. I need to set a time, a treadmill time, for one hour a day and not get sidetracked. But there is more! I need to reduce my food intake on a whole: We eat well, but I eat too much. Oh, and maybe I should stop the ice cream. I do buy it for the grandkids, but then I eat the rest.

Where am I going with this? The same commitment Angie and I have for the Lord needs to go into my health, because the Lord has directed me in it. There is no way that the Devil or his cohorts want you to partner up with Jesus. To do that will require discipline, commitment, stamina, and courage, but it is worth every bit of energy you spend. Push in, press in! Anyone can have an intimate relationship with Abba. He is waiting for you, actually longing for you, so I encourage you to make this part of your routine in your day. You will not find anyone that you could get any closer to than Jesus. This is not for the elite, the elect, the privileged, or the special: Jesus died for all of us, so that each and every person, male or female, young or old—who call on His name—can have life and have life more abundantly. After salvation, relationship is our greatest gift and part of this is abundance. Jesus stands at the door and knocks, so let Him in. It will be truly awesome. This is one lifestyle change you will never regret!

In essence,

We are to hunger and thirst after Him:

We are to have an unquenchable thirst and unfillable hunger.

We are to love the Lord with all our heart, mind, and soul.

He is to be our first love.

Chapter Eleven: Kingdom Works International

A good name [earned by honorable behavior, godly wisdom, moral courage, and personal integrity] is more desirable than great riches; and favor is better than silver and gold (Proverbs 22:1 AMP).

Many years ago (around 2002), I was seeking the Lord, and asking Him what this ministry He wanted me to launch should be called. I asked Him if it should be John Edelmann Ministries (many people have a personal ministry). I already knew I was called to ministry, and He had quickened the above scripture to me about it. The Lord told me it should be called Kingdom Works International. I thought that was a nice name but wondered why this particular name was right. I knew I was called to the nations, but why Kingdom Works International? He told me that His "kingdom works" and it is international. I was ecstatic! I thought, *What a name!* It is a good name for a ministry. A *good* name is to be chosen rather than great riches, so I sat on the name for years, waiting for the proper time for it to be launched. I waited for God's release.

If you were to use your own name that would be one thing; but when God gives you the name, and it has a direct correlation with His name and kingdom, it may take some time to see the release of that ministry. He has to make sure that it is all in line with His good name. Possessing "a good name [earned by honorable behavior, godly wisdom, moral courage, and personal integrity]" is a journey in itself. Timing is everything. When God shows us something and we are young in the

Lord or overzealous, we often jump ahead of Him and try to make it happen. In doing that, we can do the wrong thing and tarnish our own name and in some cases, God's. At the very least, what we do is out of God's timing. Hence, the Lord works on honorable behavior, godly wisdom, moral courage, and personal integrity in our lives before He releases us into full-time ministry. As He is a gracious and loving Father, He does give us tastes (or short seasons) of what is to come to help us and propel us into our destinies. For me, that was all the overseas trips. They helped prepare me for what is here now. What an awesome God!

My journey included all my wilderness experiences: years filled with trials and tests. He humbled and stretched me, shaping and molding me. I endured all kinds of trouble and pain, and often wondered what in the world was going on. I was criticized and judged, and it hurt—but it was all part of my preparation for ministry. Our gracious Father is preparing you so you can walk out your God-given call with honorable behavior, godly wisdom, moral courage, and personal integrity too. He wants you to walk in excellence and good standing. You represent His kingdom and Him—in addition to your own name. He wants that name to be well-respected. This is worth more than great riches. Some people seem to get there more quickly than others, but it has taken a long time for me. Sometimes it felt like forever; I'm a bit thick, I guess. However, here I am: *still standing*. I am standing in Him, standing strong, standing firm, and no longer standing alone (because, fortunately, I now have Angie) with a vision, a God-given vision.

Kingdom Works International is an international ministry, commissioned by the Lord. In an earlier chapter I shared how the Lord woke me up and told me to go the nations and save His people. The other day I was talking with my friends in Texas. Kim C, said to me, "John, do you remember the dream you told me about before you were commissioned?" I had forgotten, so she shared it; how could I have forgotten that? The dream was this: I saw millions of people walking up this hill (I was quite far away). I said to the Lord, "What is this? (I was hovering over them in the Spirit.) I was moved closer and I saw all these faces, but now I could see they were walking up a mountain, and all of them seemed oblivious about what was going on. Again I said, "Lord, what is this?" I was taken to the top of the mountain; and as I was hovering over this mountain top, I saw it was open and I could see hundreds and thousands just walking off the end and falling into this open pit. I saw the horror and terror on their faces as they fell. When I looked down, I could see fire: It was like a volcano, but I knew what it really was. It was the entrance into hell. I woke up, totally freaked, thinking, *What am I to do?* Two nights later was when I was woken up to the Lord and the Holy Spirit commissioning me to go to the nations.

This is the mission statement I received from the Lord Jesus, the CEO of KWI, the Chief Cornerstone. We are to reach millions and millions, tens of millions for His glory.

KWI Mission Statement:

KWI is a non-profit international ministry which has been established for the purpose of taking (or sending) the gospel to all the nations, equipping the saints, feeding the poor, helping the widows, visiting prisoners, building and/ or supporting orphanages and other established ministries (according to Matthew 28:18-20, Mark 16:15-18, Matthew 25:34-40, James 1:27, and Ephesians 4:11-12).

KWI will financially support:

1. Orphanages,
2. Established ministries and mission groups,
3. Bible colleges (internationally),
4. Child rescue programs (against slavery, the sex trade, and more),
5. Micro-loan programs (to support widows),
6. Food and water programs (locally and internationally),
7. Disaster relief programs,
8. Crusades (national and international events for taking the gospel to the nations),

9. Local and international outreaches (such as prison ministries),
10. Bible distribution (in China, Middle East, India, Indonesia, and other countries).

The funding for KWI will come from the Lord as outlined in His Word:

> Then you shall see and become radiant, and your heart shall swell with joy; because the abundance of the sea shall be turned to you, the wealth of the Gentiles shall come to you (Isaiah 60:5).

> A good man leaves an inheritance to his children's children, but the wealth of the sinner is stored up for the righteous (Proverbs 13:22).

> Give, and it will be given to you: good measure, pressed down, shaken together, and running over will be put into your bosom. For with the same measure that you use, it will be measured back to you (Luke 6:38).

Funding will also come from ideas, inventions, plans and strategies from the throne room of heaven: God causing man to give into KWI for His glory.

These are our motivating scriptures to back this vision:

> The fruit of the righteous is a tree of life, and he who wins souls is wise (Proverbs 11:30).

> The steps of a [good and righteous] man are directed and established by the Lord, and He delights in his way [and blesses his path] (Psalm 37:23 AMP).

> Trust in the Lord with all your heart, and lean not on your own understanding; in all your ways acknowledge Him, and He shall direct your paths (Proverbs 3:5-6). Commit your works to the Lord, and your thoughts will be established (Proverbs 16:3).

A man's gift makes room for him, and brings him before great men (Proverbs 18:16).

He who has a generous eye will be blessed, for he gives of his bread to the poor (Proverbs 22:9).

He who has pity on the poor lends to the Lord, and He will pay back what he has given (Proverbs 19:17).

And Jesus came and spoke to them, saying, "All authority has been given to Me in heaven and on earth. Go therefore and make disciples of all the nations, baptizing them in the name of the Father and of the Son and of the Holy Spirit, teaching them to observe all things that I have commanded you; and lo, I am with you always, even to the end of the age." Amen (Matthew 28:18-20).

And He said to them, "Go into all the world and preach the gospel to every creature. He who believes and is baptized will be saved; but he who does not believe will be condemned. And these signs will follow those who believe: In My name they will cast out demons; they will speak with new tongues; they will take up serpents; and if they drink anything deadly, it will by no means hurt them; they will lay hands on the sick, and they will recover" (Mark 16:15-18).

Then the King will say to those on His right hand, "Come, you blessed of My Father, inherit the kingdom prepared for you from the foundation of the world: for I was hungry and you gave Me food; I was thirsty and you gave Me drink; I was a stranger and you took Me in; I was naked and you clothed Me; I was sick and you visited Me; I was in prison and you came to Me." Then the righteous will answer Him, saying, "Lord, when did we see You hungry and feed You, or thirsty and give You drink? When did we see You a stranger and take

You in, or naked and clothe You? Or when did we see You sick, or in prison, and come to You?" And the King will answer and say to them, "Assuredly, I say to you, inasmuch as you did it to one of the least of these My brethren, you did it to Me" (Matthew 25:34-40).

Pure and undefiled religion before God and the Father is this: to visit orphans and widows in their trouble, and to keep oneself unspotted from the world (James 1:27).

The vision that the Lord has given us is so big that it can only be God's. Only Abba can do this. It is out of the natural realm of man. When you look at the work of leaders like D. L. Moody who founded Moody Bible Institute, Oral Roberts who founded Oral Roberts University, William Cameron Townsend who began Wycliffe Bible Translators, Catherine Booth who started the Salvation Army, William Seymour of the Azusa Street Revival, and more recently: Luis Palau, Reinhard Bonnke, Pastor Cho of South Korea, and then look back to where they started, most of them began with absolutely nothing except a vision, a dream, or a word from the Lord. Through obedience and a steadfast spirit, they persevered. For those on that list who have graduated to glory, we can look at their legacy. That is what the Lord has done. They leave behind countless testimonies of God's greatness against unsurmountable odds, and ministries in God that will continue to stand for generations. How many people told these same people that what they were going to do was impossible, ludicrous, and possibly not of God? Yet here we have some of the most powerful ministries in the world! With God's help, they completed gigantic tasks. Here is one example:

Wycliffe Bible Translators got its start when William Cameron Townsend went to Guatemala in 1917 to sell Spanish Bibles, but was surprised to find that many couldn't read them. Why? "They spoke Cakchiquel, a language without a Bible. Because he believed everyone should understand the Bible, he started a linguistics school…that trained people to do Bible translation. The work continued to grow, and in 1942

Cam officially founded Wycliffe Bible Translators."[12] It took them until 1951 to complete the first translation and the 500th was finished in 2000. Wycliffe Bible Translators has over 2,000 languages that they are still working on.[13] How wonderful! What a huge task that was and still is! And what an incredible impact it has made for people to be able to read the Bible in their own languages. And this example is just one from our list above. There are countless others.

So what was the common denominator with all these people? Every one of them stepped out into his or her call. They left the known and familiar to step into the promised land, the unknown *by faith*. Denying themselves and taking up their cross, being led by the Spirit, they walked into the fullness of their destinies, not worrying about the opinion of man but resting in the Lord, who said, "Go!" However, the biggest denominator is that each and every one *paid the price* to be where they stand today. The ones that have gone to glory to be with the Father have earned their crowns, praise the Lord. Each and every one has had to contend with the critical, the condemning, and the downright envious. The hurt caused by man is crazy. Yet these believers became more than conquerors and show this through the fruit we can see born out of their lives. Well done, good and faithful servants of the Most High. It is a journey but the rewards are awesome, here and in heaven.

> But without faith *it is* impossible to please *Him,* for he who comes to God must believe that He is, and *that* He is a rewarder of those who diligently seek Him (Hebrews 11:6).

I cannot do what the Lord has shown me. Angie can't do it either, and neither could any team working with us in our own strength; only God can do it through us. Sometimes you share your dream with people, and for the life of them they cannot see it. Only the Lord can do what He has shown us. We are but conduits to be used for His glory. Kingdom

---

12. "About Bible Translation | Christian Missionaries," Wycliffe Bible Translators, accessed March 22, 2019, https://www.wycliffe.org/about.

13. "Annual Report 2018," Wycliffe Bible Translators, 2018, accessed March 22, 2019, https://wycliffe.bible/annualreport/.

Works International is His. It will be an equipping center, an epicenter for His glory. It will be devoted to salvation, restoration, healing, and deliverance, a place where the wounded and bleeding can heal. It is for the equipping of the saints for the work of the ministry, where people's gifts can be honed and sharpened before they are sent out. We want to see a place that is flowing in the glory of God, where His presence sees people set free, healed, and transformed. A place of love, not by word but by action, where the love of Christ is tangible, felt by all, no matter who you are. Where people's gifts and callings are recognized, developed, nurtured, and encouraged, a place where Abba gets all the glory.

This can only be done in Him. This is huge: Buildings are needed, and vehicles, finances, the lot. I rest assured that if the Lord can do it for those mentioned before, He can do it for us. God is not a respecter of persons. We are all the same in His eyes. All we have to do is be willing to move when He says. He will unfold the hidden things in His perfect time. *We just need to believe, receive, and walk it out*. While writing this, Angie and I are preparing to go to America. What does this look like? We don't know all the details yet, but the Lord told us to go. He will open every door that needs to be opened and close every door that needs to be closed. About the fulfillment of prophecy, dreams, visions, He says:

> Arise [from spiritual depression to a new life], shine [be radiant with the glory and brilliance of the Lord]; for your light has come, and the glory and brilliance of the Lord has risen upon you. For in fact, darkness will cover the earth and deep darkness will cover the peoples; but the Lord will rise upon you [Jerusalem] and His glory and brilliance will be seen on you. Nations will come to your light, and kings to the brightness of your rising (Isaiah 60:1-3 AMP).

A new hour has come! The things of the past are over. The Lord is going to move in ways that man has never seen before. This last harvest will be exciting and powerful; no stone will be left unturned, no soul lost.

There is a reaping beginning like no other; the faceless and nameless generation is rising up. The ones the Lord has kept hidden until now are about to be released. Exploits beyond human comprehension will be accomplished: the greatest miracles seen by man, creative miracles will be commonplace. God's glory will be seen around the world, and it will captivate the hardest of hearts. Signs will leave man wondering and saying, "Surely God is with them!" People will be undone, speechless, and asking what they must do to be saved. Rendered helpless without Christ, there will be salvations in the streets, shops, hospitals, airports, schools, businesses, prisons—everywhere. Media will not be able to keep up with this outpouring of God's glory: It will be everywhere and continuous.

The mighty hand of the Lord is moving. Nations will have His glory sweep over them, and be transformed overnight. Can that be done? Can God really do this?

> "Who has heard such a thing? Who has seen such things? Shall the earth be made to give birth in one day? Or shall a nation be born at once? For as soon as Zion was in labor, She gave birth to her children. Shall I bring to the time of birth, and not cause delivery?" says the Lord (Isaiah 66:8-9).

Yes, He can and will. His will is that not one will perish. If we don't do it, He will have the very rocks cry out. If you are not seeing this, ask the Lord to open the eyes of your heart. This is "deep calling unto deep," and this is the heart of the Father: that entire nations sell out to Him for His glory:

> For with the heart one believes unto righteousness, and with the mouth confession is made unto salvation (Romans 10:10).

> For "whoever calls on the name of the Lord shall be saved" (Romans 10:13).

Jesus said to him, "I am the way, the truth, and the life. No one comes to the Father except through Me" (John 14:6).

Jesus sits at the right hand of the Father, looking for the ones who will say, "Send me, pick me, I will go." He is looking for an *army of uncompromising fortitude,* people who will carry His glory into the nations to reap an unprecedented harvest. Entire prisons will become born again, prisoners and guards alike. This will echo into the nations as people who have never seen freedom will be set free: mentally, spiritually, and in some cases, physically. The Lord's hand is about to move in great grace across the prisons of North America. Multitudes will be transformed.

"Therefore if the Son makes you free, you shall be free indeed" (John 8:38).

Once prisoners, now preachers: A great move will come out of Mexico through the penal system, along with amazing and life-changing testimonies from prisoners who have had encounters with Jesus in their cells—signs, wonders, and miracles will come out of the prisons and the Lord will be glorified. Some will be awed as they will say, "How could God use me?" *For when much is forgiven, much is required.* Some will be released from prison and go straight into ministry, having already been transformed; they will see signs and wonders follow their preaching. They will go on to do great exploits for the Lord. Once cartel, mafia, and gang members, they will become born-again, Bible-believing, Bible-teaching, Bible-speaking, Spirit-filled, miracle-working men and women of God, doing greater works than Jesus did. The world will stop and pay attention. And people will know God's love is for everyone—not for some, and not just for the elect or the elite. God's love is for everyone—from the president to the prisoner and the homeless, and everyone in between. So be it! Abba is ramping up! His glory is about to be released like never before. When you taste of it, you will be transformed.

Oh, taste and see that the Lord is good; blessed is the man who trusts in Him! (Psalm 34:8).

People will never be the same: The *kabod* glory, the *shekinah*[14] glory, is going to be very real in many people's lives. People will struggle to go to work, as they will just not want to leave His presence. I anticipate that the body of Christ will come to a place in which they crave to be with Jesus more than anything else; their first priority every morning will be to stop everything and come into Abba's presence, soak in His glory, and then go out into the world and infect everyone they meet with His goodness, grace, mercy, and love. If you are thinking, *John, this is kind of unrealistic*, I have to say, "I have been doing this for years— everywhere I go. It is awesome to be able to speak into people's lives and see His glory touch them. The next time you see them, they share a testimony of what has happened in their lives! To God be the glory!"

This is the most exciting time in my life. I have been waiting for what seems like a million years, an eternity, okay, twenty-plus years or so, but you know what I am saying here. When the Lord speaks to you and gives you His plan for your life, it overwhelms you. Zeal and exuberance kick in and you start running, trying to make it happen, trying to open the doors that haven't opened for years. Fill in the blank: Joseph, Moses, John Edelmann, _____. You sometimes get so far ahead that the Lord has to pull you back. You did not realize that there was a long time ahead of you. Then halfway through, you lose your zeal and sometimes your vision. *It sometimes has to die so it can be resurrected.* Then something starts stirring it again, and the vision comes back stronger than ever before. This time your zeal is even stronger, but you now have the maturity to seek Abba before you move. This time when you move, it is with the Holy Spirit. The doors open up without kicking them in (or burning them down). They just slide open without resistance, and the doors behind you close—forever. *That season is done* (and in some cases, yahoo, good riddance).

So this season, this new season, is upon me. Suddenly (twenty-plus years later, but *suddenly*) everything I have believed for, everything I have been waiting for is here and screaming at me. Everything I have

14. "Shekinah," Topical Bible: Shekinah, accessed March 23, 2019, https://biblehub.com/topical/s/shekinah.htm.

shared with people is staring me down—and suddenly it looks daunting because it is so big.

This may be happening to you too! You already know that only through God is any vision going to get off the ground, let alone be what the Holy Spirit has shown you. You are somewhat anxious even though the Word says not to be. You are secretly saying, "Daddy, I hope You got my back" and you know He does. People are watching you more now than ever before to see if this is gonna fly, or crash and burn. (You gotta love people.) Everything in you is saying, step out, you got this.

The vision of Kingdom Works International is no longer a vision, it is a reality. This twenty-plus year vision is now alive. The breath of the Lord has now breathed upon it and it is alive. The logo is done, the website is done, and our move to America is right around the corner. It's all happening. Only God.

The mission statement and mandate is in place, and Angie and I are ready, expectant, excited, exhilarated with anticipation. We have committed all of it to the Lord. He is the CEO, and we are the directors on earth, ambassadors of the kingdom of God, serving through Kingdom Works International for His glory. Amen.

The only thing we can take to heaven is souls. If we became more kingdom-focused and God-reliant, our hearts would turn to the only thing that really matters: souls.

> How then shall they call on Him in whom they have not believed? And how shall they believe in Him of whom they have not heard? And how shall they hear without a preacher? And how shall they preach unless they are sent? As it is written: "How beautiful are the feet of those who preach the gospel of peace, who bring glad tidings of good things!" (Romans 10:14-15).

What if we all went before the Lord and said, "Jesus, I want my life to glorify Your name"? *What if* we asked to be used in our sphere (whatever that may be)? *What if* we said, "Lord, I only want what You have for me. Don't let me miss anything"? *What if* we said, "Lord, I want *deep encounters* with You, that my entire life would be turned upside down. Lord, that You would rule and reign in my life"? *What if* those already in ministry were to say, "Abba, we truly want more of You! Show us Your glory, Lord, and if we are missing it anywhere, please show us. Lord, we want everything You have. Let us honor Your name and represent You well. We want to walk in the fullness of Your glory. Lord, we want to be pleasing to You in all we do and say"?

May God encourage the vision He has given you and your family as you walk it out. He will faithfully prepare you and release you. May your name be established in Him, reflecting His goodness and mercy and integrity, and bringing Him glory.

Chapter Twelve: Your Will Be Done

Your kingdom come. Your will be done on earth as it is in heaven (Luke 11:2).

What is Daddy's will? That we do not take our salvation for granted, and that we do His will and not ours. That we preach the Word in its entirety, without any compromise. Some people say that we live in different times; it's not the same now, so we need to do it differently. I think He must have anticipated that because the Word says this:

Jesus Christ is the same yesterday, today, and forever. Do not be carried about with various and strange doctrines (Hebrews 13:8-9a).

The author of Hebrews says clearly that *Jesus Christ does not change*. This is quite resounding. The same sins were alive in the days before Noah, during the time of Sodom and Gomorrah, Jesus' time, and today. Nothing has changed: Sin is sin. Some sin is against the body and some sin leads to death, and then there are abominations. If Jesus is the same, without variation of change: yesterday, today, and forever, how is it that we can think His heart or mind could change toward sin? Wouldn't that mean He died for nothing? He came to set us free of sin and generational curses. He became poor so we would be rich. He hung on a tree (the cross) and took our curses so we could be curse-less. By His stripes we are healed. Through Him we have salvation and are washed in His blood. We need to adhere to His Word, and not be led astray by "strange doctrines."

> Do you not know that the unrighteous will not
> inherit or have any share in the kingdom of God? Do not
> be deceived; neither the sexually immoral, nor idolaters,
> nor adulterers, nor effeminate [by perversion], nor those
> who participate in homosexuality, nor thieves, nor the
> greedy, nor drunkards, nor revilers [whose words are
> used as weapons to abuse, insult, humiliate, intimidate, or
> slander], nor swindlers will inherit or have any share in
> the kingdom of God. And such were some of you [before
> you believed]. But you were washed [by the atoning
> sacrifice of Christ], you were sanctified [set apart for God,
> and made holy], you were justified [declared free of guilt]
> in the name of the Lord Jesus Christ and in the [Holy]
> Spirit of our God [the source of the believer's new life and
> changed behavior] (1 Corinthians 6:9-11 AMP).

What do we say then? Why are churches today watering down the Word? Angie and I just watched a couple of documentaries. In one, a very well-known pastor said "once saved, always saved"! I am not sure of that. Jesus said in Matthew:

> Not everyone who says to Me, "Lord, Lord," shall enter
> the kingdom of heaven, but he who does the will of My
> Father in heaven. Many will say to Me in that day, "Lord,
> Lord, have we not prophesied in Your name, cast out
> demons in Your name, and done many wonders in Your
> name?" And then I will declare to them, "I never knew
> you; depart from Me, you who practice lawlessness!"
> (Matthew 7:21-23).

This pastor went on to say he believed homosexuals would also go to heaven. That is not what the above verse says. And God's Word does not single out the practicing homosexual, but also the "sexually immoral, the idolaters, the adulterers, the effeminate [by perversion], the thieves, the greedy, the drunkards, the revilers, the swindlers." This is God's Word, not mine. God loves the person, but He hates the sin. That kind-of sounds like there ain't gonna be any sin in heaven. Many focus on homosexuality, but what about the one who is pointing the finger at the homosexual but they are practicing adultery? We need to back up and reread God's Word. It also clearly says that those who get saved and stop practicing the sin that had enslaved them (homosexuality or anything else) shall see the kingdom. The Word is the Word, and that Word became flesh:

> And the Word became flesh and dwelt among us, and we
> beheld His glory, the glory as of the only begotten of the
> Father, full of grace and truth (John 1:14).

Another pastor we watched said he believed people did not need to hear that they were sinning, since they already knew it. He went on to say they needed to be mentored or encouraged. I have a problem with that too. The Bible says it a little differently:

> Now the Spirit expressly says that in latter times some will
> depart from the faith, giving heed to deceiving spirits and
> doctrines of demons, speaking lies in hypocrisy, having their
> own conscience seared with a hot iron (1 Timothy 4:1-2).

Some people can get so entrenched in their sin that *they do not know* they are sinning anymore because their conscience has been seared. Many people are sincere in their beliefs, *but they are sincerely wrong*, and so firmly set in their wrongdoing that they cannot see the hurt they are causing others. We need to tell them they are sinning out of love; we cannot allow people to wallow in their sin. If we do, shame on us! We need to stand in the Word of God! It is the *only way*—just as Jesus is the only way to the Father. We need to see brothers and sisters (saved and unsaved alike) set free and growing into the new creations they were meant to be. We need to see them walk in freedom, with the chains of bondage broken off them. He who the Son sets free is free indeed. I, for one, do not want to stand before the judgment seat, answering God as to why I did not preach the Word in its entirety, especially since doing that will cause some people to go to hell.

I am not concerned with people's opinions, criticisms, or judgments about me. I am only concerned with what the Lord thinks about me. In the end, I stand before no man; I stand before the Lord and must be accountable to Him for what I did or didn't do, what I said or didn't say. I will not water down the Word for anyone, nor will I compromise the Word of God. I will never be part of a seeker-friendly church, or a church run by man and not the Spirit. We have become such a politically-correct society that people are becoming frightened to share the Word of God or take a stand for it.

I have spent time in third-world countries, sharing my word from the Lord about living an extreme life with Jesus, so I find this ironic. In some of these countries they stand for the Lord so uncompromisingly that some are martyred for their faith in Jesus. Seriously, that is happening. They will not water down the Word; they live it unto death. In some countries they are shot or have their heads cut off (these are lucky ones); others have gas poured on them and are burnt to death. Yet, they will not compromise. They will not deny the Word or Jesus as Lord and Savior. That is amazing.

I have been amazed at the determination of the people in some of the places I have been about their walk with Jesus. One of the most outstanding things I ever saw in Indonesia was the hunger and thirst for God these believers had in spite of their poverty and all their troubles. Their desire for God outweighed everything. Their joy was exuberant, just leaping out of them. They were proud of Jesus: This quality seems to be lost in the more developed countries.

Your Will Be Done on Earth as in Heaven

What is His will? *Abba wants us to walk out an uncompromised life in Him*, as lights in the darkness. Through our lives and the Word, people are drawn to Him. How? They should be able to see the peace, joy, and love we have in the Lord, and know we have something they don't. We should stick out because we're different. We are to be vessels for the Holy Spirit to use at His will—to the glory of Jesus and the Father.

The Father's will is to have a personal relationship with all of us, not a superficial one. He wants a relationship so deep and intimate that people around us are drawn to us by His supernatural love—one that cannot be manufactured by any man, but only comes through the Holy Spirit. It is not judgment, criticism, or finger pointing that will see people saved, it is a pure and undefiled love. It is love, grace, and admonition that brings people out of sin and transforms them. Abba's will is that we, as His people, chase Him with everything we have, so we can be transformed by Him and go out into the world to preach the gospel and partner with Him in reaping a harvest. God's will is that we do this as worship, and we worship Him in spirit and truth.

His will is that we all become born-again, Spirit-filled, Bible-believing, Bible-speaking men and women walking in the supernatural gifts God has given us. We should be so full of the Holy Spirit that we can't contain ourselves—*we have to give it away*. Everywhere we go, we should leave His glory as a deposit in someone's life. Our relationship with the Trinity (the Father, the Son, and the Holy Spirit) must be so apparent in us that it oozes out into everyone we meet and into every situation we encounter. Our world in Jesus is full of great joy, peace, and love: That cannot come from man, and that fruit leaves wonder in its wake. It's all about relationship and unity with the Father:

> Until we all reach oneness in the faith and in the knowledge of the Son of God, [growing spiritually] to become a mature believer, reaching to the measure of the fullness of Christ [manifesting His spiritual completeness and exercising our spiritual gifts in unity]. So that we are no longer children [spiritually immature], tossed back and forth [like ships on a stormy sea] and carried about by every wind of [shifting] doctrine, by the cunning and trickery of [unscrupulous] men, by the deceitful scheming of people ready to do anything [for personal profit]. But speaking the truth in love [in all things—both our speech and our lives expressing His truth], let us grow up in all things into Him [following His example] who is the

> Head—Christ. From Him the whole body [the church, in all its various parts], joined and knitted firmly together by what every joint supplies, when each part is working properly, causes the body to grow and mature, building itself up in [unselfish] love (Ephesians 4:13-16 AMP).

Hmm, seems pretty clear: Unity is the order of the day. What does unity bring?

> Behold, how good and how pleasant it is for brothers to dwell together in unity! It is like the precious oil [of consecration] poured on the head, coming down on the beard, even the beard of Aaron, coming down upon the edge of his [priestly] robes [consecrating the whole body]. It is like the dew of [Mount] Hermon coming down on the hills of Zion; for there the Lord has commanded the blessing: life forevermore (Psalm 133:1-3 AMP).

For where there is unity, God commands a blessing. So what is up with prejudice and bigotry? Look at every tribe, every creed, every race, and every color, and take away all color (red, yellow, brown, black, white, or any other color). We have such an incredibly creative God. When I listen to people who have been blessed to visit heaven and able to take it all in, they describe the colors there and the sheer beauty of heaven. They say it is full of vibrant colors and they try to describe the deep richness they saw. People cannot fully recount what they really saw, but they do their best. They always finish by saying that they cannot do it justice with words. I have heard many, and they all saw similar things. So here is my point: If Abba has ordained heaven in an array of exquisite colors, and that is who He is, why would He not do the same on earth? Actually, in every part of creation? Well, He has. There is spectacular beauty all over! God finds beauty in color!

Look at the human body! If one race or all races were built, manufactured, or let's say, created differently, then you could say, "Wow, dude, that is strange indeed." However, this is not the case. Every human being has every body part in common: heart, lungs, kidneys, liver, eyes, ears, blood, and so on. And every body's system works the same way. There is no variation in function: none between different colors or creeds. Every one of us bleed the same color. Whoa, what? Yep, we all have this in common, whether we want to believe it or not. So then what is prejudice? Simply put, prejudice is ignorance, and ignorance breeds more ignorance. If someone does not stand up and say that enough is enough, this ugliness will continue and worsen. It is appalling that it even exists in the church today or ever did in the past.

> **Prejudice:** Preconceived opinion that is not based on reason or actual experience; harm or injury that results or may result from some action or judgment. (Synonyms: preconceived idea, preconception, preconceived notion. Or: detriment, harm, disadvantage, damage, injury.) [15]

Since God made heaven so beautiful that it is indescribable in its color and majesty, would He not do the same with earth? It is His good pleasure to array His people in the beauty of color. Who are we to come against His creation or judge it? The problem of prejudice exists everywhere, but this not ought to be. Abba created us for His glory. We are to come together as one and worship Him for His goodness and mercy, not be at war with one another. This is a ploy of the Devil: divide and conquer, separate and split. When we allow prejudice to rule, we are really letting Satan rule, the father of all lies.

> Therefore submit to God. Resist the devil and he will flee from you. Draw near to God and He will draw near to you. Cleanse your hands, you sinners; and purify your hearts, you double-minded (James 4:7-8).

I was once sent by the Lord to a church in Louisiana to pray for the senior pastor. At the time, this pastor was on the board of his denomination, and there were (I can't remember exactly) 300 or

---

15. "Prejudice | Definition of Prejudice in English by Oxford Dictionaries," Oxford Dictionaries | English, accessed March 08, 2019, https://en.oxforddictionaries.com/definition/prejudice.

600 churches in the group. I felt that the Lord wanted me to preach throughout the denomination to speak about having an extreme walk with Jesus and to see freedom released throughout this movement. I prayed for the senior pastor and he was healed (this was documented); but after speaking with one of his associate pastors later, it was decided that I should not be allowed to preach in their church because I had been divorced and I remarried. After this meeting, I found out that this same associate pastor had just disowned his own daughter because she had married a born-again, Spirit-filled, Bible-believing, Bible-preaching, mighty man of God who was also black. She had married a strong Christian pastor, a great man of God who was an African-American! When I heard this, I almost fell out of my chair. Would you not be ecstatic, overjoyed if your child married a God-fearing man, a true man of God? Would color matter to you? In this case, it did. When I thought later of the church itself, I realized that everyone in it was white! After the senior pastor was released from the hospital with a new heart and no need for an operation, he and his wife took us out for dinner. They picked us up, and we were driving down the road when I overheard the pastor's wife say, "Look at those porch monkeys!" I turned and looked, and she pointed at a family of African-Americans (or let's say Americans) sitting on their front porch! We were shocked, but it wasn't over yet. Next she said, "Yeah, and I can't stand those Chinks (Asians) either." My first thought was, *Wow, you are the pastor's wife! Are you for real? Where is the love? Where is the honoring other people—all made in His image?* Forget unity! You can't walk in unity if you don't have any love. This is so wrong. Don't even get me started. This church allowed me to minister to people at the end of a service only. They stood there and said to one another, "Can you feel the power that is coming off him (the power is the Holy Spirit)?" But they would not let me preach. The Lord sent me there with a word, but I could not bring it; so when it was time to leave, I shook the dust from my feet and moved on.

> And whoever will not receive you nor hear your words, when you depart from that house or city, shake off the dust from your feet. Assuredly, I say to you, it will be more

tolerable for the land of Sodom and Gomorrah in the day of judgment than for that city! (Matthew 10:14-15).

I don't care what color you are! Prejudice and bigotry are rooted in fear and ignorance. That way is not God's heart. He created all men and women equal and in His image. He created all men and women to worship, praise, and honor Him for who He is. We all need to pray:

> Create in me a clean heart, O God, and renew a steadfast spirit within me. Do not cast me away from Your presence, and do not take Your Holy Spirit from me (Psalm 51:10-11).

I pray this often. It is a good way of saying to the Lord: "Search my heart; and if there is anything in me that is displeasing to You, get rid of it. I give You permission to excavate my heart. Take out everything and anything that displeases You." I truly believe prejudice of any kind displeases the Lord. If you agree, read this, and then read it again out loud as a prayer. May the Lord have His way in our hearts!

> *Father, I pray right now in the name of Jesus, and I boldly enter into the court rooms of heaven (Your throne room). Lord, create in me a clean heart, O God, and renew a steadfast spirit within me. Do not cast me away from Your presence, and do not take Your Holy Spirit from me. Lord, You know my heart and if there is anything in me that displeases You, please bring it to the surface. I do not want anything in me that displeases You. My heart is to love everyone equally, as You love. Lord, please give me Your heart, so I can love as You love, and I can give as You give. May I forgive as You forgive. Oh, Lord, search my heart, try my anxieties, and show me if there is anything that is keeping me from walking in the fullness of Your glory. Show me, Lord. I thank You that You hear me, and I believe and I receive everything I have prayed for. May I walk in Your love, Lord: Love with unity. Amen.*

And above all things have fervent love for one another,
for "love will cover a multitude of sins" (1 Peter 4:8).

We are not to take stands as one denomination against another denomination or color against color: It was never God's purpose or desire to have that. Never! We are all to be one body under one God (not in a one-world-order sort-of way, but in a God-is-in-charge-and-orders-everything-perfectly sort of way). Jesus died for everyone: black, white, brown, red, olive, and everything in between; He went to the cross for the Jew first, and then the Gentile (that covers everyone else). How do we get this so fouled up? After the cross, the Jesus movement was called the "way." Everyone who believed was added to the movement, and there weren't any different denominations or sects. The book of Acts was written as the foundation of the church. What was done then is still supposed to be happening now because Jesus is still exactly the same today as He was then! Jesus is the unchanging God. Can you imagine a united body that comes together to worship the One and only true God in Spirit and in truth? There will be no denominations, colors, or creeds: All that will be nonexistent. Jesus is coming back soon, for this exact thing, His body. How exciting!

In the meantime, it is the Father's will that we are busy doing what we are called to, the work of the ministry, fulfilling our destinies. One weekend Angie and I went to a church that the Lord directed us to attend. We asked one of the regulars what denomination it was, and they said it was non-denominational. They said they were sort of Pentecostal, but not overboard. I find it funny how people describe what they are—and more importantly what they are not. The service was interesting: The worship was dry, the sermon was great, and at the end they had a time of tongues, interpretation of tongues, and prophecy (I had not seen this in church for years). It was very orderly and felt religious. We listened carefully to the people there (and they were wonderful people); some had been there for twenty-plus years. It seemed no one was really doing anything for God, but they came every week, listened to a sermon, and returned home. We are called to much more that this—all of us. I am not judging or condemning anyone here. The point is that we can get so caught up in "doing church" that we miss the fact that there is much more we could open the door to if we allowed the Holy Spirit freedom to move. Every one of these people were friendly and welcoming.

> I assure you and most solemnly say to you, anyone who believes in Me [as Savior] will also do the things that I do; and he will do even greater things than these [in extent and outreach], because I am going to the Father. And I will do whatever you ask in My name [as My representative], this I will do, so that the Father may be glorified and celebrated in the Son. If you ask Me anything in My name [as My representative], I will do it. "If you [really] love Me, you will keep and obey My commandments (John 14:12-15 AMP).

Jesus said we would do greater things than He did! Jesus went around healing everyone! What could be greater than that? Nevertheless, He said we would do greater things: creative miracles perhaps. Praying for people to be filled with the Holy Spirit is one of the greatest things we should do after salvation. Everything else after that: healing, deliverance, tongues, raising the dead, signs, wonders, and creative miracles are also blessings. Our lives have not been truly impacted until the Holy Spirit dwells within us. This is when the transformation truly begins. As I think back over my life, I can see how He has brought me from glory to glory through the Holy Spirit. Remembering where I began compared to where I am today blows my mind. I thank God for everything. What a gracious God!

God's grace is the empowerment to move forward. Grace is never to be used as a stopping place or a license to sin. It is the empowerment to rise above the situation and leave it behind. Empowerment is to be set *free* of bondage, addiction, and sin, and walk in grace. I feel like jumping out of my skin! Is God good or what?

> **Empowerment:** Authority or power given to someone to do something; the process of becoming stronger

and more confident, especially in controlling one's life and claiming one's rights. (Synonyms: acceptance, acknowledgment, approval, consent, freedom, liberty, permission)[16]

Abba's will is for us to grow, be empowered, and move forward. We should be continually seeking more of Him so we can reach the fullness of our potential. One thing I have learned is that in God, there is always more—more of Him to gain, more of us to give, more to be stretched. Being shaped and molded can be a painful, even ugly process at times, but when we are truly submitted to the Lord, saying, "I am Yours, and I want Your will to become my will. I want everything You have for me," grace takes over.

God has no greater desire than to have our whole heart. He doesn't want to just be a *part* of our life. He wants to *be* our life, He wants our full and complete devotion, and all the affections of our heart. That is His will. He wants strong relationships with us just as He had with Moses, Joshua, Joseph, Daniel, and David! We can just add our names to that list. Press in! I encourage you to go deeper! You will never be disappointed with Jesus.

I can't get past this idea that we will do "greater things" than Jesus did. Stop and take that in: Jesus went around healing *all*, not some. When Jesus was baptized, the Holy Spirit descended upon Him, and then He went around preaching that the kingdom of God was at hand with signs, wonders, and miracles following Him.

And here is the mind-blowing part: When you become born again and Spirit-filled, this is what has just happened: That same Holy Spirit who filled Jesus now dwells in us! This is the very same Holy Spirit who was with God the Father when He said, "Let there be light" and light appeared. When the Father said, "Let there be a firmament," land appeared, and when Abba said, "Let the land separate from the waters,"

---

16. "Empowerment | Definition of Empowerment in English by Oxford Dictionaries," Oxford Dictionaries | English, accessed March 08, 2019, https://en.oxforddictionaries.com/definition/empowerment.

the Holy Spirit did it. When Abba said, "Let Us create man in Our own image," the Holy Spirit did it. Again, that *same Holy Spirit* now dwells in us: the same Holy Spirit who raised Jesus from the dead! The *dunamis*[17] (explosive power) of the Holy Spirit lives within us now too!

Meditate on this truth! I have known this for years, but recently the Holy Spirit has been giving me a deeper revelation of what this really means. Take this in! That same Holy Spirit who shaped and created the earth and everything in it, raised Jesus from the dead, and now works great signs and wonders through all those who have asked Him to come and dwell within them—*He lives in you!* Yes, it's true! If we are Spirit-filled, we will do greater things than Jesus, for His glory. We are entering a time of seeing some of the greatest creative miracles ever recorded in history. It is only through the Holy Spirit and in the name of Jesus to the glory of the Father that these things will be done.

Our biggest problem is that we do not fully understand who dwells inside of us or realize His power. We say, "Greater is He that is in me, than he that is in the world," but do we really understand that the same power that hung the stars, sun, moon, and planets, and formed the earth and everything in it, actually dwells *in us*? That's astounding!

Take some time to ponder it for a while. This is really powerful. If we can grasp this, there is nothing we cannot do—within the will of Jesus. We limit the Holy Spirit with what He can do through us because we do not understand the fullness of His power. When we get a revelation of His power, we can walk in this same great power and authority. Creative miracles will follow. God wants to flow through us to do great things; and as we are completely submitted to Him, we become vessels He can use in this way. Praise the Lord!

Summing up: It is Abba's will that we walk in the fullness of the Holy Spirit and fulfill our destiny in Him.

---

17. James Strong, "1411. Dunamis," Strong's Greek: 1411. δύναμις (dunamis) -- (miraculous) Power, Might, Strength, accessed March 23, 2019, https://biblehub.com/greek/1411.htm.

What if we said, "Lord, show me Your will for my life"? *What if* we all were to seek spiritual maturity, and be everything He has called us to be? *What if* we could see that all men and women were created equal and we took a stand against prejudice and bigotry? *What if* we united together to fulfill His will?

For those who read this *that do* have prejudice beliefs, you need to consider this: *Eternity is forever.* If you can't stand another people group here on earth, how will you do with them in heaven? It won't be segregated there, and *eternity is forever!* And there is one other problem: I'm not sure that a bigot will even enter heaven! That's God call, but it is food for thought.

What if we could get past ourselves and all our thoughts, feelings, and agendas? *What if* we could get on the same page as the Lord and do His will? Time is running out. *Jesus is coming, and soon.* An extreme life is doing the will of the Father, and I pray all of us could come into the fullness of His will.

Chapter Thirteen: Don't Settle For Second Best

What is settling for second best? Good question! Second best is not God's perfect will for your life. Many people have settled for second best because the best is harder. To walk in God's best comes at a price. The biggest cost is to deny oneself, take up the cross, and follow Jesus, being led by the Holy Spirit. This involves an array of different things: family, work or career, land (or country), agendas, motives, personal plans, and much more. God's destiny for you will truly outweigh what you have to give up, in time. Knowing that should mean that this is not such a big deal, right? Wrong! We get so caught up in life and so comfortable that when we look at stepping out into the fullness of what the Lord is calling us to do, it looks terribly daunting. I mean, seriously: giving up the known for the unknown? Who does that? It seems to make so much more sense to step into each day as we have planned it, as opposed to walking by faith.

Yes, second best can definitely be easier—but you will never be truly content there. In the back of your mind there will always be the "what ifs." *What if* Peter, Matthew, Luke, and John had all decided this was all too hard? Well, in actual fact, they did. After Jesus was put in the tomb, they didn't pick up the ball and run with it. They went back to what they knew. Peter and his brother Andrew, and James and his brother John went out fishing again until Jesus came and got them a second time. They were eyewitnesses to all the miracles Jesus had already done, and He had spoken this over them well before His death:

> Then He said to them, "Follow Me, and I will make you
> fishers of men" (Matthew 4:19).

They knew the call upon their lives, and yet they went back to what they used to do: That was a *second-best* decision. Let's jump back to that moment for a second. Picture yourself there, watching and listening to the boys for a minute. It may have gone something like this:

Peter: "Well, that's it then! It's all over."

Andrew, looking at his brother: "Well, what do we do now?"

John: "Wow, man, I did not see this coming! This is not what I expected at all!"

James: "Hey, you guys wanna go fishing?"

All: "Hmm. Well, we don't have anything else to do, do we?

Another perhaps: "Was that a waste of three-and-a-half years?"

So glumly they go off. Later they are out fishing and Jesus shows up. He doesn't condemn them, judge them, put them down, or run them into the ground for missing it. He gathers them up, loves them, feeds them, and gets them all fired up again. He sends them to the upper room and says, "Hang in there, I've got something for you, and don't leave (this time)."

Here is the point: Many of us have missed it, and in some cases, terribly. "Rejoice in the Lord always. Again I will say, rejoice!" (Philippians 4:4). We serve a God of the second, third, and seventy-seventh (actually 70 x 7) chances. If we truly repent for missing it, ask forgiveness for all our mistakes and sin, He is quick to forgive us. If we turn from the ways that displease Jesus, everything can change in a heartbeat. The love of Abba far outweighs any of that. Daddy is quick to get us back on track.

> "For I know the plans I have for you," declares the Lord,
> "plans to prosper you and not to harm you, plans to give
> you hope and a future. Then you will call on me and

come and pray to me, and I will listen to you. You will seek me and find me when you seek me with all your heart. I will be found by you," declares the Lord, "and will bring you back from captivity" (Jeremiah 29:11-14).

This is the Lord speaking in this passage. He has plans for all of us, and I mean, everyone. If we don't know what His plans are for our lives, all we have to do is ask. Once we ask, He will tell us, and then it is up to us to choose to fulfill that calling. Thankfully we do not have to do it on our own. He is right with us all the way.

And once we know, what an opportunity! But we should also think about the cost. We must be careful what we ask God for, as He may give it to us. We should be very careful what we tell Abba we will do for Him, as He may hold us to it.

I want to share what happened recently when Angie and I were talking with a friend. The Lord had placed him upon our hearts for days. We were interceding for him, as he is called to an extreme walk with Jesus in China (mainland China). This is Abba's first, and best, place for his life, not second-best. In China, Christians are persecuted for their faith; some are put in prison, others just disappear, and some are put to death. Horrible, but true. As I write, I have been texting back and forth with our friend while he is at the airport on his way to China. What a mighty man of God! He has taken the call of God to the fullness of whatever God has planned. A month ago I had a couple of prophetic words for him. I had not talked to him for almost two years before that. I shared the word via e-mail, and it was 100% accurate. A few days later as we were interceding for him, Angie saw him overseas. She saw him being persecuted and eventually dying for his faith. He called. As we were talking, I told him that Angie had a vision while we were interceding for him. Naturally, he asked what she saw. How do you tell someone something like that? I told him that she saw him ministering overseas and that because of his passion, he would serve unto death if need be. He said, "Yes, the Lord has already shown me that too." I know this will not happen on this trip as he will have a huge harvest first, but it may in the future. Settling for second best in his life would mean he would not go, but stay somewhere safer, go to church, and pray that this people group would be saved somehow. He is prepared to go at any cost, but in his case, it could be the ultimate price.

We may not all be called to this, but many around the world are. Jesus paid the ultimate price for each and every one of us. He went to the cross, His chosen place, His first place. No one before or since could have fulfilled this destiny. At one point, He even said this:

> Saying, "Father, if it is Your will, take this cup away
> from Me; nevertheless not My will, but Yours, be done"
> (Luke 22:42).

What if Jesus had said, "Okay, Daddy, I have thought this through, and I don't wanna do this. I would like to go back to being a carpenter. These guys will be okay down here. Somehow or other it will turn out." Thank God that Jesus was able to fulfill His mandate and take the keys to life and death from hell. He paid the ultimate price for our salvation and reconciliation to the Father. He died once for all, and now sits at the right hand of the Father. He could never ever have settled for second best.

There are so many people who have settled for second best. I have considered it many times. Walking by faith is no easy task. You have the pressures of life, work, family, people around you daily. You have to trust the Lord for everything, and that is easier said than done. When the Lord tells you to step out in faith and walk by faith, retire from the Babylonian system and step into the kingdom, this action is often greeted with sometimes unbelievable responses: The unsaved don't get it at all (and that is okay), but surprisingly, a lot of Christians don't get it either. The first thing out of a Christian's mouth is often this verse:

> For even when we were with you, we commanded
> you this: If anyone will not work, neither shall he eat
> (2 Thessalonians 3:10).

I find it funny that this is the only part of the verse mentioned when they speak. The context of the whole passage is really saying something else. It is referring to people who do not work because they are lazy. It is not talking about people in ministry—and ministry in itself can take up more than an eight-hour day.

> Let the elders who rule well be counted worthy of double honor, especially those who labor in the word and doctrine. For the Scripture says, "You shall not muzzle an ox while it treads out the grain," and, "The laborer is worthy of his wages" (1 Timothy 5:17-18).

> So also [on the same principle] the Lord directed those who preach the gospel to get their living from the gospel (1 Corinthians 9:14 AMP).

There is much more written about how the Lord will bless those who forsake all to preach His gospel:

> The fruit of the [consistently] righteous is a tree of life, and he who is wise captures and wins souls [for God—he gathers them for eternity]. If the righteous will be rewarded on the earth [with godly blessings] (Proverbs 11:30-31 AMP).

If we are truly called by God and we want to walk in the fullness of His call upon our lives, we have to believe that He will provide for us. It is His glory to provide for us. He will meet our every need.

> And my God will liberally supply (fill until full) your every need according to His riches in glory in Christ Jesus (Philippians 4:19 AMP).

The truth is that if you have decided to "take the bull by the horns" and stop running from the call on your life, not settling for second best and run with Jesus instead, Abba has no choice but to have your back. His Word is higher than His name, He said, "If God is for you, who can stand against you?" The Devil can try, but he is a defeated foe. When you rise up in the fullness of Jesus' authority and power, nothing—but nothing—can stop you. All of hell can (and probably will) come against you, but it can only ever buffet you, *not stop* you. We can do all things through Christ who strengthens us.

Settling for second best can have detrimental effects. Many years ago, a friend came to my house. He was all excited and said he was getting married. I had met his girlfriend, and she was a nice person, but he was a worship leader and she was still unsaved at the time. She did give her life to the Lord, but at this time she was still smoking dope and not really into the church thing like he was. He asked me and my wife what we thought. My wife looked at him and said, "Mate, you only want to get married so you can have sex. That's not a good enough reason." He smiled. I felt the same thing and told him that I did not believe this girl was the right one. I urged him to wait on God, trusting that He would bring the right one, His first choice, to him. Well, there is nothing worse than when someone asks for advice and then doesn't take it. They got married, had a child, then had a very rocky and volatile relationship, which ended a few years later. This affected his ministry, and opened doors for depression and more. Had he waited, the Lord would have given him the perfect woman, someone who would have had his back, and supported him in life, work, marriage, family, and ministry, pushing him gently to be everything he was called to be in Abba, rather than tearing him down and belittling him.

Many of us settle for second best, and in some ways, it is not our fault. We are born and trained up in a world system, in addition to the monetary (or Babylonian system) too. We are told what to think and say, how to act, and how to be. We are set up like this from birth. The funniest thing I ever heard is that Christians are brainwashed! That's hilarious! It's the world system that is brainwashed, not us! Christianity is completely opposed to the world's system. The world's way is to go with the flow and not question why. You are just supposed to do what is expected of you. Meanwhile, that system is filled with corruption and wickedness! If being a Christian is to be brainwashed, I welcome it.

Having lived the world's system, I love having a washed brain, the mind of Christ instead.

Here's another example of not settling for second best: When you know the Word, you will not settle for anything but what the Word says. In 1993, I came to Australia with two of my sons. My wife at that time and other three sons came three months later. We were living in Werribee. I was having my morning time with the Lord when my wife came to me with my youngest son, Jordan. Jordan was only about five or six months old at the time. She showed him to me, and said, "I think there is something wrong with him. His hands, feet, and lips are all red and swollen. I think we need to take him to the doctor." So off we went. The doctor thought he had a virus, and saying that he looked dehydrated, told us to give him lots of water and bring him back if he wasn't better in three days. Three days later, Jordan looked worse—much worse. We went back to the doctor. He said, "I have never seen anything like this in my life. Take him to the Royal Melbourne Children's Hospital and don't stop for anything! This is serious."

We took off down the road, heading for the city. I was praying, asking God to step in. Then I heard this very clearly (not audibly), but loud and strong just the same:

> Is anyone among you sick? Let him call for the elders of the church, and let them pray over him, anointing him with oil in the name of the Lord. And the prayer of faith will save the sick, and the Lord will raise him up (James 5:14-15).

We were at the Hoppers Crossing junction, and I had two choices: The first was to go straight, hit the freeway, and head to the hospital, and the second was to turn left and go to the church. This scripture was resonating in my head and repeating itself over and over. I turned left, and my wife began yelling at me, asking where I was going. I explained what I heard. She responded by loudly reminding me that the doctor said not to stop. She was terribly worried. I told her I had heard from God; and as I drove toward the church, my heart was desperately hoping

Pastor Graham or someone, anyone, would be there. I pulled into the driveway and the parking lot was full: There were cars everywhere. Rushing in, I found Pastor Graham and explained why I was there. He looked at me and said: "Today every elder, leader, and pastor is here!" (It was first time in the church's history that they had done this too. It was a new building and they had all taken a day off work to pray in the new vision for the church!) If you didn't know God, you might think this was just coincidence, but it gets better.

Everyone in the building came out to the parking lot, and Pastor Graham anointed Jordan with oil and prayed over him, with everyone else praying in the Spirit, and then we were back on the road again and heading for the hospital in Melbourne. It was very vocal in the car for a bit, so I prayed under my breath; it was wiser. One of us wasn't up for the God-thing at the moment. The next thirty-five minutes seemed to take forever, but during this time I kept thinking, *What are the chances of all those people being at the church? Apparently pretty good!* God, only God! You have to remember that I was very young in the Lord; this was all new to me.

We finally got to the hospital and took Jordan in. The first nurse looked at Jordan and started calling for more doctors and nurses; she seemed a little worried. By this time they had Jordan on a bed in the hallway with about four or five nurses and four doctors all looking at him in amazement. They were clearly baffled. Nobody (and I mean nobody) knew what was happening to Jordan. Abba's timing is impeccable. Another doctor came strolling down the hall, casually looked over shoulders and asked what everyone was looking at. The other doctors responded by telling him that they didn't know, as they had never seen this before.

This doctor looked at my son again. We found out later that this doctor was visiting from London, and was only here for three days. He had just been returning from lunch—*and just happened to stop.* God's timing!

My wife and I were standing right there watching all this, and my wife was beside herself. I was just taking it all in. The new doctor knew what was wrong and immediately took charge. He said, "This is Kawasaki disease, a deterioration of the heart. We do not know how it is contracted and there is no cure. It was diagnosed by a Dr. Kawasaki and named for him." (I knew it had to be something demonic, being a Harley man myself). This all happened at the end of 1993 or early 1994. We were asked if they could take photos of Jordan for the medical journal, as they had never seen a case this advanced. Most children died long before. Then the English doctor spoke to our doctor again: "You should prepare the parents," he said, "because this little guy won't be going home."

We were taken into the doctor's office and told to make preparations as Jordan had no more than seven days left to live. They took X-rays of Jordan's heart. It was falling apart. As you can imagine, my wife was in tears. The doctor asked what we wanted to do, so I asked for a few minutes with my wife. He left and she asked me, "What are we going to do?" Well, my spirit rose up and I said, "First, we are going to reject the words of man and his diagnosis. I honor doctors and respect their training and commitment, but I heard the word of the Lord. Jordan is healed. I believe it and receive it. He will live and not die." My wife could not even grasp that right then. The whole thing was just too overwhelming for her.

For the next few days I stood on the word, and Pastor Graham had the church praying. Three days went by and nothing had changed. They did more X-rays on the fourth day, nothing. I pressed in. I was not going to settle for second best or the word of man because I had heard from God. The fifth day was not much better. On the sixth day, they took X-rays, and said, "Hang on! Something changed!" On the seventh day we took Jordan home! He had a brand-new heart! There was no operation, other than a Holy Ghost operation. Last month Jordan turned twenty-six. He works full time, goes to the gym, and has a lovely fiancée named Bree. They just had a baby girl, Ariah. God had another plan for his life.

This was the first miracle I ever saw. I have seen many since; but to me, this was earth shaking. I had been pinned to the ground and I felt the filling of the Holy Spirit: mind-blowing. But *seeing Jordan healed when trained professionals were saying it was over and there was no hope, was incredible.* It was a true miracle. The tests showed that his heart was deteriorating, but God healed it! The Lord has continually blown me away over the years with amazing things which leave me saying, "Only God!"

This was all documented and will go into another book, along with many other documented healings. Why did I share this in this chapter? Because I was a fairly new believer at the time and I was faced with two options: Man's or God's. God's way is always better. It may not look like the most obvious way, but it will turn out best. In this case, God proved Himself to me. He has done many amazing things since, and I am in awe of this truly-incredible God we serve. How blessed are we to have the Creator of the Universe want to hang out with us? If I would have settled for second best and listened to the opinion of man, Jordan would have been put in a box. I am not trying to be callous, but that is what would have happened. I love my boys and want the best for each of them.

Settling for second best is not the will of the Lord. Abba has an extreme life with Him prepared for anyone who will take Him up on it. Jesus said He came to give life and give it more abundantly. I don't think He was referring to a mediocre life in which we go to work, spend a little time with the family, go to church on Sunday, and then repeat that over and over again. Because I had an intense life prior to the Lord, a mundane life does me in. Well-meaning Christians will say, "Come on, John, it is okay to be out there a little, but you are pushing it." I thought, *God, I can't be boring! That is not who I am. You didn't make me to just sit around. I want to conquer the world (a metaphor), and plunder hell to populate heaven.* I was blessed when I read *Wild at Heart* by John Eldredge. All men should read this book—saved or unsaved. What a book! The title says it all. It gave me renewed peace about who I am. This is how the Lord created me and this is who I am. If this is who God created me to be, I ain't letting no one change me; many have tried. I am God's creation made to bring Him glory, and that is what I will do.

In this, my heart is for one thing: that everyone (men, women, and children) would go before the Lord with this simple prayer, believing it and receiving it with all their heart:

> *Abba Father, am I walking in what You have called me? Am I where You want me to be? Or have I settled for second best? If I am not doing what I am supposed to be doing, give me the grace to get there. Do what You have to do in me to have me be the person You created me to be—for Your glory, Lord. If You have called me to walk an extreme walk with You, and my heart is not in it, please change my heart. I want to fulfill everything You have for me. Thank You, Lord! I pray this in Jesus' name. Amen.*

Be blessed! Reap the harvest you were put here to reap. I truly believe everyone is to reap a harvest: this could be one or millions. We are to be a beacon of light to this dying world. We are not to put this light under a basket (or hide it); it is for the world to see. There is no retirement in the kingdom of God. We can be used by the Lord to our very last breath and no one is too young. Jesus said that out of the mouth of babes came perfect praise. Jesus can use young children as well. Abba wants to use *you*. It is up to us. I pray that you would rise up into the fullness of the call upon your life. There is nothing more fulfilling than leading someone to the Lord and doing His will. You will never feel more exhilarated or alive than when you are walking with Jesus in an extreme walk led by the Holy Spirit. Life doesn't get any better!

> Most assuredly, I say to you, he who believes in Me, the works that I do he will do also; and greater works than these he will do, because I go to My Father (John 14:12).

What if we all prayed, "Lord, I refuse to settle for second best. I ask that You would take me to the place, where I can serve You in the fullness of the call upon my life"? *What if* we told that Devil to stop telling us it was too hard, that we can't do it, and that it was not for us and rebuked him in Jesus' name instead? *What if* we said, "Lord, here I am! I am ready to serve You with everything I have! Use me, Lord"? *What if* we prayed, "Lord, not My will be done, but Your will be done in my life. I want to walk an extreme walk, glorifying Your name. I want to do the things and say the things You ask me to do and say. That alone is extreme. I want to live in complete obedience to You, Lord"?

Chapter Fourteen: And Suddenly

A nd *suddenly*" a touch from heaven is all you need, and you will never be the same. A life turned upside down, in a twinkling of an eye. One hundred and twenty people in the upper room and *suddenly* a rushing wind and they are all Spirit-filled and speaking in tongues (a prayer language).

> When the Day of Pentecost had fully come, they were all with one accord in one place. And suddenly there came a sound from heaven, as of a rushing mighty wind, and it filled the whole house where they were sitting. Then there appeared to them divided tongues, as of fire, and *one* sat upon each of them. And they were all filled with the Holy Spirit and began to speak with other tongues, as the Spirit gave them utterance (Acts 2:1-4).

Not one of their lives were ever the same again. Ironically there were 500 in the upper room in the beginning. However, with the pressures of life, hobbies, family, lack of commitment, or whatever, over the fifty days of waiting, some lost heart or doubted. 380 people left and missed this great outpouring of the Holy Spirit. (That is not to say some didn't get filled later, but to be there for that moment of a *suddenly* when it was documented that fire was seen upon them: how wonderful that had to have been!) Words synonymous with *suddenly* are *unexpectedly*, *unforeseen*, *immediate*, and *immediately*.

Suddenly: Quickly and unexpectedly. (Synonyms: immediately, instantly, promptly, unexpected, abruptly.)[18]

We have now truly entered a time of *suddenlies*. You may have been waiting for five, ten, twenty years for the dreams and prophecies to appear and then, bang, they will be in your face. It will be a time of the natural meeting the supernatural, a time of seeing everything come together. A time in which you are *suddenly walking out* what you used to dream about. Not only will the dream be tangible, but supernatural finances will also be there to support the dream. It will be a time of awe and wonder, a time of gratitude and thanksgiving. *Suddenly* everyone who thought you were crazy will be more shocked than you. *Suddenly* it will be time to run with your God-given vision. Batter up, it is time to hit a home run, to run the course set before you. *Suddenly* you are walking in the fullness of God! He has got your back and nothing will stop you: This is your time to glorify the Lord! Amen. Despite all odds—even after people told you to give up, to quit, to pack it in—you stood and *suddenly* Daddy, Himself has shown up to say, "Well done, go get'em!" *Suddenly* you are off.

Suddenlies can come so fast that we can miss them! This is why we need to be in tune with the Holy Spirit, so we do not miss what is coming.

> However, when He, the Spirit of truth, has come, He will guide you into all truth; for He will not speak on His own authority, but whatever He hears He will speak; and He will tell you things to come. He will glorify Me, for He will take of what is Mine and declare it to you (John 16:13-14).

Again, this all comes out of intimacy. Time spent with Abba will allow us to really know His voice so we do not miss a *suddenly*. Time

18. "Suddenly | Definition of Suddenly in English by Oxford Dictionaries," Oxford Dictionaries | English, accessed March 08, 2019, https://en.oxforddictionaries.com/definition/suddenly.

is short. Many have been waiting for years and years to be released into their destinies, to see the hand of the Lord show up and launch them out into the deep. I am one of them. Today I prophesy over anyone reading this who has been waiting for such a time as this:

> *I decree suddenlies to be released over Your people, Lord, to see Your people arise and shine for Your glory. Father, that Your glory would rise upon them, that Your people would move in a greater level of glory, reap greater harvests, and carry a greater mantle of healing, and a greater mantle of deliverance. May they move in greater levels of Your dunamis power, so that signs, wonders, and miracles would be released. I prophecy that witty ideas, inventions, and strategies will be released. May ministries be birthed and released, and ministries already in place set on fire for Your glory, Lord. May there be suddenly after suddenly in Jesus' name. Amen. (So be it!)*

There are eighty-seven occurrences of *suddenly* in the Word, and since *suddenlies* are in the Word of God, we can expect them. They are coming. We have entered a time of suddenlies: non-stop suddenlies. But what about the next day? *What if we were so close to Abba that when we prayed, it all came together the very next day?*

When all of what is needed comes the next day, it is an amazing thing. Acts 10 recounts that kind of story. When God shows up, things happen. Because it is so appropriate to this subject, I have included the entire chapter below. It is worth reading.

> [1]There was a certain man in Caesarea called Cornelius, a centurion of what was called the Italian Regiment, [2] a devout man and one who feared God with all his household, who gave alms generously to the people, and prayed to God always. [3] About the ninth hour of the day he saw clearly in a vision an angel of God coming in and saying to him, "Cornelius!"

[4] And when he observed him, he was afraid, and said, "What is it, lord?"

So he said to him, "Your prayers and your alms have come up for a memorial before God. [5] Now send men to Joppa, and send for Simon whose surname is Peter. [6] He is lodging with Simon, a tanner, whose house is by the sea. He will tell you what you must do." [7] And when the angel who spoke to him had departed, Cornelius called two of his household servants and a devout soldier from among those who waited on him continually. [8] So when he had explained all these things to them, he sent them to Joppa.

[9] *The next day*, as they went on their journey and drew near the city, Peter went up on the housetop to pray, about the sixth hour. [10] Then he became very hungry and wanted to eat; but while they made ready, he fell into a trance [11] and saw heaven opened and an object like a great sheet bound at the four corners, descending to him and let down to the earth. [12] In it were all kinds of four-footed animals of the earth, wild beasts, creeping things, and birds of the air. [13] And a voice came to him, "Rise, Peter; kill and eat."

[14] But Peter said, "Not so, Lord! For I have never eaten anything common or unclean."

[15] And a voice spoke to him again the second time, "What God has cleansed you must not call common." [16] This was done three times. And the object was taken up into heaven again.

[17] Now while Peter wondered within himself what this vision which he had seen meant, behold, the men who had been sent from Cornelius had made inquiry for Simon's house, and stood before the gate. [18] And they

called and asked whether Simon, whose surname was Peter, was lodging there.

¹⁹ While Peter thought about the vision, the Spirit said to him, "Behold, three men are seeking you. ²⁰ Arise therefore, go down and go with them, doubting nothing; for I have sent them."

²¹ Then Peter went down to the men who had been sent to him from Cornelius, and said, "Yes, I am he whom you seek. For what reason have you come?"

²² And they said, "Cornelius the centurion, a just man, one who fears God and has a good reputation among all the nation of the Jews, was divinely instructed by a holy angel to summon you to his house, and to hear words from you." ²³ Then he invited them in and lodged them.

On *the next day* Peter went away with them, and some brethren from Joppa accompanied him.

²⁴ And *the following day* they entered Caesarea. Now Cornelius was waiting for them, and had called together his relatives and close friends. ²⁵ As Peter was coming in, Cornelius met him and fell down at his feet and worshiped him. ²⁶ But Peter lifted him up, saying, "Stand up; I myself am also a man." ²⁷ And as he talked with him, he went in and found many who had come together. ²⁸ Then he said to them, "You know how unlawful it is for a Jewish man to keep company with or go to one of another nation. But God has shown me that I should not call any man common or unclean. ²⁹ Therefore I came without objection as soon as I was sent for. I ask, then, for what reason have you sent for me?"

³⁰ So Cornelius said, "Four days ago I was fasting until this hour; and at the ninth hour I prayed in my

house, and behold, a man stood before me in bright clothing, [31] and said, 'Cornelius, your prayer has been heard, and your alms are remembered in the sight of God. [32] Send therefore to Joppa and call Simon here, whose surname is Peter. He is lodging in the house of Simon, a tanner, by the sea. When he comes, he will speak to you.' [33] So I sent to you immediately, and you have done well to come. Now therefore, we are all present before God, to hear all the things commanded you by God."

[34] Then Peter opened his mouth and said: "In truth I perceive that God shows no partiality. [35] But in every nation whoever fears Him and works righteousness is accepted by Him. [36] The word which God sent to the children of Israel, preaching peace through Jesus Christ—He is Lord of all— [37] that word you know, which was proclaimed throughout all Judea, and began from Galilee after the baptism which John preached: [38] how God anointed Jesus of Nazareth with the Holy Spirit and with power, who went about doing good and healing all who were oppressed by the devil, for God was with Him. [39] And we are witnesses of all things which He did both in the land of the Jews and in Jerusalem, whom they killed by hanging on a tree. [40] Him God raised up on the third day, and showed Him openly, [41] not to all the people, but to witnesses chosen before by God, even to us who ate and drank with Him after He arose from the dead. [42] And He commanded us to preach to the people, and to testify that it is He who was ordained by God to be Judge of the living and the dead. [43] To Him all the prophets witness that, through His name, whoever believes in Him will receive remission of sins."

[44] While Peter was still speaking these words, the Holy Spirit fell upon all those who heard the word. [45] And those

of the circumcision who believed were astonished, as many as came with Peter, because the gift of the Holy Spirit had been poured out on the Gentiles also. [46] For they heard them speak with tongues and magnify God.

Then Peter answered, [47] "Can anyone forbid water, that these should not be baptized who have received the Holy Spirit just as we have?" [48] And he commanded them to be baptized in the name of the Lord. Then they asked him to stay a few days (Acts 10, italics for emphasis mine).

You could get a whole bunch of sermons out of this chapter, but here are seven of the main points:

1. *"Your prayers and your alms have come up for a memorial before God":* Abba Father hears our prayers, so never give up pressing into Daddy, asking, seeking, and knocking, for when He moves, it will come upon you *suddenly.*

2. *"Now send men to Joppa, and send for Simon whose surname is Peter. He is lodging with Simon, a tanner, whose house is by the sea. He will tell you what you must do":* When we spend time with the Lord, He speaks to us. He not only speaks to us, but He speaks clearly and concisely. Get your head around this: Abba (via an angel) said, "Now send men to Joppa (the place or city), and send for Simon whose surname is Peter (the name, the exact name). He is lodging with Simon, a tanner (He is staying with Simon and his job is a tanner, not to be mixed up with Simon next door who is a goat herder, and he lives by the sea). "He will tell you what you must do": (instruction will come as to what to do next). Come on, this is over the top! Cornelius is told to send people to Joppa, looking for Peter, who is staying with Simon, a tanner, who lives by the sea, and this Peter guy will to tell you what to do next! Sounds like God speaks to people quite specifically, doesn't it? If we are intimate with Him, He will tell us exactly what to do—just like Cornelius.

3. *"Then Peter opened his* mouth and said: *'In truth I perceive that God shows no partiality'":* Everyone is the same to God. There is no partiality with Him—all men are the same. He will speak to anyone who has relationship with Him.

4. *"To Him all the prophets witness that, through His name, whoever believes in Him will receive remission of sins": All* who call on the name of Jesus will be saved and their sins forgiven, no matter what. Amen.

5. *"While Peter was still speaking these words, the Holy Spirit fell upon all those who heard the word. And those of the circumcision who believed were astonished, as many as came with Peter, because the gift of the Holy Spirit had been poured out on the Gentiles also":* The Holy Spirit is for everyone who believes and He pours Himself out freely.

6. *"For they heard them speak with tongues and magnify God":* Yes, this is for today. Jesus is the same yesterday, today, and forever! He is still filling His people with His Spirit as He did then.

7. *"'Can anyone forbid water, that these should not be baptized who have received the Holy Spirit just as we have?" And he commanded them to be baptized in the name of the Lord":* We are to be baptized into the Father, Son, and Holy Spirit, be Spirit-filled, born-again Christians who preach the Word of God everywhere we go—going into our world to the glory of the Lord.

This was the plan of the Lord. The Lord prepared and spoke to Peter as Peter was praying. Later when Peter was waiting for lunch and decided to seek the Lord, he went into a trance, and the Lord told Peter what to do before it happened. When these guys showed up at his door, Peter already knew Abba was in this. He went with them so that Jesus' name would be glorified and the kingdom expanded. God is so far ahead of us that we may as well be standing still. Our plans were written before the foundation of the world. We just need to enter into a greater level of intimacy with Him. As we do, we begin seeing the Next Day and the Following Day experiences, and we no longer have to wait six months, twelve months, and five years. It will happen *suddenly*.

The Lord is looking for people who will walk in the *suddenlies* for His glory. The amazing thing about the *suddenlies* is this: When He speaks, you have to move or you will miss it. As fast as a *suddenly* shows up, it can be gone. Cornelius heard and sent his men, and the *next day* Peter heard and was ready for what was coming. The *next day* Peter moved on what he was told, and then *the following day,* he was exactly where he was supposed to be: at the right place, at the right time, meeting the right people, and doing exactly what he was supposed to be doing. And how does God respond? The Lord opens the door to the Gentiles: one Spirit, one vision, cities apart, two men who were intimate with the Lord—and *suddenly* their worlds are turned upside down. Cornelius, his family, and friends are *suddenly* born-again, baptized, Spirit-filled, tongue-speaking Christians. Peter and his dudes are blown away! Remember: "those of the circumcision who believed were astonished"! They witnessed that Abba was calling in the Gentiles, that He was not partial, that He loved everyone equally, not just Jews, that Jesus died for all who would call upon His name, and that through the name of Jesus, anyone could be saved.

Suddenly we are about to see a wave of glory sweep over the world. *Suddenly* we will see a harvest like never before, and *then suddenly* we will see the Rider on the white horse, His name is Faithful and True! Jesus will return for His body, and then *suddenly* Jesus and the body of Christ will be gone. The Word says that Jesus will return in a twinkling of an eye. That is as *suddenly* as anything can get: here, then gone. *Are you ready? Will you be ready?* Will you be moving in the things you are called to? Walking in the *suddenlies* of this time?

Suddenlies are the coolest thing; you have such high expectancy. You know something is about to happen, but you are not sure how it is going to happen. Even so, you are sure that you are sure; it is going to happen. Then when it does happen, it is truly amazing, to say the least. The funny thing is that when you are waiting on a *suddenly* from God, it rarely, if ever, happens the way you thought it would. I don't know how many times I have been believing for something (even now), waiting on a *suddenly,* believing I know the answer is on the way. And it comes from a completely different source, or in a different manner than I expected, one I could not have ever imagined. The way the Lord speaks and provides sometimes leaves me more than a little surprised, even shocked. Just like the disciples must have been at different times, I find myself thinking, *Wow! I didn't see that coming! That's not the way I would have done it.* Nonetheless, God's way always seems to be better than our way.

Here is another *suddenly*: People are going to get saved and *suddenly transformed* the same day. (This is what happened to Angie). In a heartbeat, a lifestyle will be transformed and changed. People will grow into spiritual maturity in months instead of years. They will get saved and then *suddenly* be out preaching, with miracles following those transformations. God will be getting all the glory, Abba will be opening doors for these people that others waited twenty-plus years for. Is this awesome or what? This will not just be a few select or special individuals either, it will happen to 1,000s and 10,000s. There is no time to waste! Jesus is coming! The Lord is moving across the nations right now, looking for those He can call and equip quickly. It will seem like it happened overnight. This is going to happen in the Muslim world too: 1,000s of people will be *suddenly and radically* transformed overnight. It is actually happening there already. The Lord is moving. China is about to see a *suddenly* of biblical proportions. The hand of God is going to sweep through that nation. This move will even touch those in power in the government. Russia, look out! The glory is about to hit *suddenly*. The walls will come down. Internal walls will be shattered, just smashed, and the freedom of the Spirit will be released. People will be saved by the thousands, tens of thousands, hundreds of thousands. *Suddenly, suddenly, suddenly!* What a time to be alive!

I want to share a *suddenly* that happened to me some time ago. I was living in Brisbane and the Lord told me He wanted me back in Melbourne. I was working in real estate at the time, and I didn't want to go back to Melbourne, as it can be cold there in the winter. Brisbane's weather is awesome, summer or winter. Anyway, I didn't want to go. I've worked in real estate off and on for the last twenty years, and overall I had done fairly well. Because I wouldn't go, God made it so I could list properties but would not sell anything. I had six contracts on one house, and each one fell away and came to nothing. It was so frustrating. Finally, I realized God was not going to bless me because I was being disobedient, and said, "Okay, Lord, I will go." Immediately I got a seventh contract that went through on that house! However, because of my earlier rebellion, once I paid off my bills and it was time to move, I had no money. (Can you say *stretch*?). So Abba gave me the date and I organized the movers. They came, picked up the furniture, and told me they would see me in three days. I am thinking, *Cool, that will give time for the Lord to provide because I don't have any money!* Here's where it gets a little tricky. My family is ready for this road trip, but I had checked the bank account that morning at seven and there was nothing there. I had been asking the Lord for a $1,000, figuring that was what it would take to get the seven of us, with a stopover, meals, fuel, and so forth, to Melbourne. Someone suggested I check it again. It was now ten in the morning.

Suddenly there was money there: $750! I'm thinking, *Well, that's not quite what I asked for*, but at the end of the trip, I still had fifty dollars. We got there in two days. Again I was thinking, *Okay, this will give God time to provide our deposit money and our first month's rent. Then I have another day for the furniture money, right?* Remember, if God has called it, He will pay for it. We got to Melbourne and someone put us in a motel for the night, as we were now believing (well I was) for the deposit and rent money. Then I got a call and the guy said, "Hey, we had a great run and we're here early! We're parked outside your house." I said, "Man, we don't get the keys until tomorrow! I will be at the house around ten tomorrow." Now I am thinking, *Whoa, God! You really gotta move here!* Now I am believing for the money for the furniture guys too. No big deal for God, right. What's $7,000 to Him?

The next day I got up early to check the bank account. Now the money for the deposit and rent were there, praise the Lord. Who knows this is not a time to panic? It was a time to do the next thing you can do. So off we went to the real estate office. We signed the lease, paid the deposit and the rent, got the keys, and headed to the house. Well, we got to the house, unlocked the door, and had a quick look at it (as this was the first time we had seen it). Here in Australia it is very hard to rent a house without a prior inspection, but God, in His favor, got us the house, sight unseen, with no deposit, and the lady had held it for us for two weeks! Does this sound like God to you? After seeing the house, I came out to the front to unload the vehicle and the furniture guys arrived. One man opened the back of the semi-trailer, pulled out the ramp, and the driver said, "Well, as soon as we get paid, we will unload."

Suddenly, another guy pulled up, climbed out of his truck, walked up to me, and said, "I can't stay. I have to get to work." He handed me an envelope, jumped back into his truck, and left. (Does God use people to get His will done? Absolutely. He doesn't need to use people if they are not willing, but He enjoys partnering with us. His will shall be done on earth as it is in heaven—with or without man.) And yes, in the envelope was the exact amount of money we needed: not a penny short, not a penny over. The one thing I have noticed in my walk is that it always seems that the Lord shows up or provides at the very last minute. He's never late and never early. Most trips overseas have been the same: All the money comes just before I leave. Although this is the way for many people, others seem to have everything they need way in advance. Strange indeed. That house was a stretching house; we were there for four years, sometimes barely. Did my faith get stretched and strengthened over that time? Yes! We got two or three eviction notices, and each time—and at the very last minute—God came through. People gave because the Lord told them to give; most people do not just give money away. People were sowing into the vision God had given me, just as I had sown into others:

> Give, and it will be given to you. They will pour into your lap a good measure—pressed down, shaken together, and running over [with no space left for more]. For with the standard of measurement you use [when you do good to others], it will be measured to you in return (Luke 6:38 AMP).

When we understand the law of giving and give tithes, offerings and the sowing of seeds unto the Lord, Luke 6:38 kicks in. For the sake of explanation, I will share this because I can already hear people saying, "The Word says you do not let your right hand know what your left hand is doing, and you are to do things in secret." Yes, it does say that, but I have given cars, a motorcycle, and furniture away. I have paid people's hotel bills and other expenses, fed the poor, bought food, clothing, and shoes for families, paid people's deposits and rent or airfare, and even paid people's drug debts to protect them. I have sown tens of thousands (if not more) dollars into churches, people, and ministries and wherever else the Lord told me to sow. You give expecting nothing in return,

> Now [remember] this: he who sows sparingly will also reap sparingly, and he who sows generously [that blessings may come to others] will also reap generously [and be blessed]. Let each one give [thoughtfully and with purpose] just as he has decided in his heart, not grudgingly or under compulsion, for God loves a cheerful giver [and delights in the one whose heart is in his gift]. And God is able to make all grace [every favor and earthly blessing] come in abundance to you, so that you may always [under all circumstances, regardless of the need] have complete sufficiency in everything [being completely self-sufficient in Him], and have an abundance for every good work and act of charity. As it is written and forever remains written,
>
> "He [the benevolent and generous person] scattered abroad, he gave to the poor, His righteousness endures forever!" (2 Corinthians 9:6-9 AMP).

Abba loves a cheerful giver! If you do not give cheerfully with purpose or you give without love, keep it in your pocket! There is no blessing on a gift or offering taken from you because you felt forced or manipulated. If your heart is not in it, don't give. Am I being harsh? No, I am sharing the Word. I was born a giver, and I will be a giver until I am in glory. God made me this way, and I will always be a giver. Do I give to receive? No, I give as I am led by the Lord. I do it with a grateful heart and I love how I feel after blessing a person, a church, or a ministry. This does not only refer to finances either. This also refers to our time, labor, or whatever the Lord asks of us. We love the unlovable, feed the poor, support the orphan, and help the widow.

> "It's not how much we give but how much love we put into giving." — *Mother Teresa*

> "We make a living by what we get. We make a life by what we give." — *Winston Churchill*

Laborers need to eat; they need a roof over their heads, traveling money and so forth, so they can do the work of the Lord. God provides, but Abba chooses to use us, so we are to give with a cheerful heart.

So here we are.

Suddenly, the time has come upon us. Angie and I are going to America. North America, it is time! All the years of preparation, shaping, testing, and proving have come to a close, and now the Lord is saying, *"Get ready, you are about to go over. You are about to cross over into the promised land, the land I have promised you. North America will burn. My Spirit will cause North America to burn, and I will raise up a beautiful bride out of her. It is America's time to shine, to be a light to a dying world. I will cause her to repent and turn from her ways; and I will raise this land up out of the ashes, and she will be glorious once again. No one who comes against her will succeed. I have called her, she is Mine, says the Lord. My hour for America is now! Watch and see what I will do in this hour. My hand is upon her. I love America and her people. I will cause the greatest revival America has ever seen to flow in her, the greatest revival America or the world has ever seen. America, rise and shine, for your time has come, I am about to loose My glory upon you. It will be wave after wave, and nothing and no one will be able to stop what I am about to do. My love for you is too great to leave you as you are. Arise, arise, arise, says the Lord! I will move across America like I did in the upper room:* **suddenly, suddenly, suddenly!** *Be ready, here I come. I am coming soon."*

Years ago, we traveled from Malaysia to Kuala Lumpur down to Singapore and over to Batam Island, Indonesia. We ended up at a church in the middle of nowhere. We had to climb a steep hill to get to the church because there was no road to it. I was looking out at the people, and thought, *They all know each other; they are all saved.* Even so, the Holy Spirit said, "Have an altar call!" I thought, *that's odd.* But I did an altar call and only one woman came up. She had never asked Jesus into her heart; she had never given her life to the Lord. Now this is the crazy part: She was roughly seventy odd years old and had been going to this church for twenty years! It was an honor to lead her through the sinner's prayer, and then pray for her. The pastor was blown away. He said she had been coming there for a long time and he never knew she wasn't saved. I learned something very important at this church: *Never ever* assume people are saved, and *always do an altar call.* Just because everything looks good on the outside, it doesn't matter. It is the heart that needs the transformation. Someone could be sitting beside you for years and be unsaved.

So if you have got this far and have never asked Jesus into your life, I urge you to really consider reading this prayer, and then praying it out loud. As the Word says, we are to make the confession with our mouth. Jesus said,

> Jesus answered him, "I assure you and most solemnly say to you, unless a person is born again [reborn from above—spiritually transformed, renewed, sanctified], he cannot [ever] see and experience the kingdom of God" (John 3:3 AMP).

If you have never asked Jesus into your heart, He is waiting for you. He wants to be your King of Kings, your Lord of Lords. Abba has a hope and a future for you. Asking Him into your life is the best thing you could ever do. Please pray this:

Father, I pray to You right now in the name of Jesus. I believe that Jesus is Your Son. Jesus, I know that I am a sinner, and I ask that You would come into my heart and become my Lord and Savior. I ask that You would forgive me of all my sins and transgressions. I surrender everything to You right now and ask You to take over my life. I thank You, Jesus, that through my confession I am now born again. My sins are washed away according to Your Word. I am a new creation in You; all things have passed away and behold, all things are new. Jesus, I ask that the Holy Spirit would fill me now! Holy Spirit, I give You permission to come and dwell in me! Use me, Lord, for Your glory. In Jesus' name, I am now born again, filled with the Spirit, a new creation. Thank You, Lord. Amen.

For those who have asked Jesus into their lives and who are born again, but are not Spirit-filled, it is only through the Holy Spirit that we can do what we are called to do. We all need to be born again and Spirit-filled to walk in the transforming power of God. If you are not sure if you are Spirit-filled, most likely you are not.

Tongues, interpretation, and all the gifts of the Spirit are for today; but more importantly, being filled with the Holy Spirit is essential. You cannot complete the fullness of your call without the filling of the Holy Spirit. I ask that you would pray this:

Jesus, I am born again and I ask in Your name that the Holy Spirit would come and dwell in me. Holy Spirit, please come and reside in me. Transform my entire being, and I ask that as a sign of being Spirit-filled, I would receive the gift of tongues, Your holy language. Holy Spirit, I receive You now and ask You take over my life. Your will be done on earth as it is in heaven for my life. Holy Spirit, I want to fulfill everything written in my book to Your glory! Thank You, Holy Spirit. Thank You, Father, and thank You, Jesus. Amen.

Is this real? I was asked to go to an insurance company in Texas by Reverend Weldon Mackay (an awesome man of God) to minister to a certain woman who was the office manager. Rev. Weldon had been telling her about me and she wanted to meet me. I had already had my five hours in the Spirit (praying in tongues) that day, so we went in. As I was talking to her, the Holy Spirit started giving me words of knowledge about her, her husband, and family. She was kind-of blown away. She had given her heart to Jesus, but that was it. *Suddenly*, I was prophesying over her and I asked if I could pray for her. I lifted my hand to place it on the top of her head and I said, "Holy Spirit, release Your glory upon her now, fill her to overflowing." She fell over (was slain in the Spirit).

Suddenly she was speaking in tongues as she laid on the floor. When she got up, she was truly overwhelmed. First she had an encounter with the Holy Spirit. Then she was speaking in tongues, another first. She started crying because she was so moved and touched by the Lord. She had never experienced that before. I have seen many people get Spirit-filled: They are transformed. It is wonderful, and *suddenly* they just start speaking in tongues. I have seen it over and over.

I am constantly before the Lord saying, "Lord, I want everything You have for me. There is more, so much more, Lord, and I want it all." I bless everyone who has read this book and I hope and pray it has stirred you to want and expect more. The Lord has a great deal more for anyone who will ask. Here comes your *suddenlies!* Bless you!

So *what if* we all said, "Lord, I am all in"? *What if* everyone reading this was to say, "Lord, this book has stirred my heart to believe for more"? *What if* you said, "Lord, the things John has spoken about sound good, but maybe, just maybe, they're a little out there. I'm not sure, but if what he is saying *is of You, show me*, Lord"? *What if* you said, "Lord, show me the truth! Lord, is there really an extreme life for me with You?

If so, I want it"? *What if* you could believe for *suddenlies*, and *suddenly* after *suddenly* became your everyday?

> *Lord, show me Your glory. I want to walk and live in Your glory! I want to be transformed and used by You. Amen.*

I end this book, hoping, believing, and praying that it has done what it was meant to do, which is to stir the hearts of all who have read it to believe for more. There is always more, no matter who you are or where you are. Abba has so much more for everyone who will press in: deep calling unto deep. If you are in deep, go deeper; if you are only in up to your ankles, wade out to your neck. Jesus will go with you.

There is a harvest to be reaped! The Lord is doing a new thing, and it is going to be spectacular. The level of glory about to be poured out upon the earth is going to be amazing. His glorious power will be poured out and we will see the masses saved like no time in history. Let's all become history makers! The time is short, so let's make every minute count.

For those who say, "John, this is all good, but I can't do what you're doing," I say, "God can use you too. If the Lord can use me, He can use anyone." The awesome thing is that He will use everyone who will say, "Lord, pick me. I don't know how this works, but I am willing to be used for Your glory!" That's all it takes.

I bless each and every reader and pray this book has had a great impact and stirred your spirit to seek God's heart. May you be hungry and thirsty for Him and draw continually closer, walking happily in His will for your life. Live your book!

About the Author

Originally from Canada, John traveled to Melbourne, Australia, with his wife and five sons, where he had a radical encounter with Jesus in 1993. An angry young man, John went from a history of abuse, drugs, and crime to a new life in Christ. He has traveled into six nations as an evangelist, and served as a leader in the church as well as in missions work and outreaches. Moving greatly in prophetic evangelism, he and his wife, Angie, live by faith. John has seen many lives come into God's kingdom, transformed for His glory. The Lord has instructed them to go to North America for the next stage of their journey, and they are very excited to see what the Lord will do with them there. John believes that a life sold out to Jesus is the only life worth living: extreme living or nothing! *What if we all surrender to His will?*

John can be contacted at:
admin@kingdomworksinternational.org

CPSIA information can be obtained
at www.ICGtesting.com
Printed in the USA
LVHW040138051020
667929LV00001B/87